REJECTED SILVER

RICK NEHRT

WORDS MATTER
P U B L I S H I N G
OUR WORDS CHANGE THE WORLD

Words Matter Publishing
P.O. Box 1190
Decatur, Il 62525
www.wordsmatterpublishing.com

ISBN 13: 978-1-962467-43-8

Library of Congress Catalog Card Number: 2024947848

Chapter 1

IN THE BEGINNING, God created the heaven and the Earth. This was the creation of the whole universe. There was nothing out there—no planets or stars, no sun or moon, no man, no angels, nor beasts of the Earth. Darkness was everywhere; the only light would have radiated from God himself. Why did God create the heaven, the Earth, and the whole universe as we know it? Because God is the ultimate love story, creating and making all humanity and his glorious creation for all to see. It is the purest and most perfect kind of love story. With a love so pure and so strong, sharing that love is the greatest gift of all.

The knowledge and understanding of the word of God is amazing. When you read it all, every single word, front to back, taking it at its word and true meaning in a proper context, you know with 100% certainty it was divinely inspired. It is a grand mystery written thousands of years ago. It had to be written in such a way that things are not revealed until the proper timing, context, and meaning. If you have any reservations about the nature of God, take a trip away from the city lights, day or night. Find a quiet place and just look around. Be honest with yourself—don't deny what you can see, hear, and smell. Put your cell phones down. Take some time and just look at his grand and glorious creation. The gravity of it all is breathtaking.

I'm going to try and explain the creation story from a rational point of view, staying in the confines of scripture. I hope to clear up some of the confusion about the creation of our universe because if you do not understand the beginning in proper context and the way it was intended, then none of the scriptures will make any sense. You see, it was no accident or random act. If one piece of the Bible puzzle is put in the wrong place, the whole book will not make any sense to you. The word of God could not be updated or changed in any way. That is why the Bible is written in a mysterious way—everything has to be revealed at a certain place and time.

Remember, God knows to write in a mysterious way to keep us on our toes, ever reaching, growing, and expanding our knowledge, ever searching to solve the grand mystery of the Bible. You may think that the mystery of the word of God was only written on our behalf. No, it is to keep the evil one, Satan, off his game. He is searching for clues, trying to manipulate the whole world with his evil schemes, for he knows in the written word his time is short.

In the beginning, all of the creating was done by the spirit of God, from Genesis 1 to Genesis 2:4. These verses are so critical to the beginning of it all. Drop all preconceived thoughts, what you have been taught, or what you've heard. God chose a very specific way to create the universe and the world as we know it. God could've created man to act as robots—acting, talking, moving, and doing as God commanded. It would've been a cold and unassuming type of existence. That would've been the easy thing to do, the path of total control, not free will. Knowing the consequences of that glorious act, God chose free will. The world and all of humanity would've been a boring and robotic place to live in.

In the beginning, God chose to create everything by his divine spirit, and all things he created were spirit-breathed. Some came from the Earth, some came from water, some came from nothing—out of the thin air. One of the most amazing things is the different natures of God.

God manifests himself as God, the Lord God, and the Lord throughout the Bible. That divine act is very critical to the grand mystery of the creation story.

I'm going to list some of the mysterious things God created: the creatures of the sea, the birds, and the great beasts of the earth that came from the ground or the water by the spirit of God. Being created that way is why we have a fossil record of our great creatures of the land, sea, and air. I am one of those people who do not deny science, especially when it bolsters the word of God.

Chapter 2

THERE ARE THOSE in the church who believe in a young Earth. I may have fallen into that camp years ago until I started reading and researching the word of God. That narrative, in any way, shape, or form, is not possible. When I started on this quest, I had to drop all my preconceived thoughts and what I was taught. I soon realized everything I thought I knew about the creation of all humanity was wrong. I did not like that—it made me angry. The word of God was written in such a way that certain things are not revealed, not known, until the right time in history. That time is now.

The Eden of Adam spans millions, perhaps even billions, of years. I will explain—it is quite shocking. I realize that the written word of God has to be taken in proper context, wording, and in the proper timing. In the beginning, God created the heaven and the Earth, not the heavens. After I read the Bible in the NIV, they put, "In the beginning, God created the heavens and the Earth." At the time the Bible was translated from King's English to NIV, they did not know the gravity of that. Heaven, not heavens, is significant. This is not a generic term. There are no generic words in the Bible. The wording should not have been changed; it was put there for a reason. I will explain how important that was a little later on.

When God created the creatures of the sea and the great beasts of the Earth, it was a testament to His love and power. We have to remember, at this point in time, pre-Adam, there was no rain on the Earth. There was water and streams that watered the ground, but no rain—that would come a lot later. The placement of plants that the dinosaurs would have eaten was conducive to areas where plants grew out of the ground but not from seed. God gave all the beasts and the birds of the air everything that had the breath of life in it, green plants for food. This tells us that all the great beasts and birds were vegetarians in the beginning. I will explain the reasoning behind this a little later in the book.

What I'm going to do right now is reveal one of the most shocking parts of the creation story. When I discovered that in Genesis chapter 1, verses 26 through 28, the creation of man was the very first creation of the human race, the sons of God, everything started to fall into place. I discovered how profound and shocking it is.

Chapter 3

THE AMAZING REVELATION of the Sons of God being the primeval race and the mystery behind that is one of the greatest and most mysterious things in the Bible. Without that revelation, none of the scriptures will make sense, and that was all by design. You have to keep in mind that God knows the beginning to the end, and that is why the Bible is written in a mysterious way. The pre-race, the Sons of God, were to remain hidden until now.

The creation of man in Genesis chapter 1, verses 26 through 28, states: "And God said, 'Let us make man in our image, after our likeness: and let them have dominion over the fish of the sea, and over the fowl of the air, and over the cattle, and over all the earth, and over every creeping thing that creepeth upon the earth.' So God created man in his own image, in the image of God created he him; male and female created he them. And God blessed them, and God said unto them, 'Be fruitful, and multiply, and replenish the earth, and subdue it.'"

You will notice that there is no mention of Adam in this context, and everything was created by the spirit of God. Since all of the creating was done by God in the spirit, this is one of the most critical things God did. The narrative that was set years ago, that the first humans created were Adam and Eve, is nothing further from the truth. I will explain in detail later on in the book. The unintended consequences of that narrative have caused some in the biblical community to make the jumps. "My mom and dad used to say all the time, that the Sons of God are not true, not possible, and very dangerous." I will talk about all this in detail later on in the coming chapters.

I'm going back to the beginning, where it all started. Please keep in mind and understand that when the Bible, the word of God, says "in the beginning," that's what it means. When God created the heaven, then God stated God started with the heaven; this is the base of operations, and later on, it will be the home of the angels and where our celestial bodies revolve.

When God created man, he created them in the image of God, the Sons of God—a living, breathing spirit, a spirit body spoken into existence. When God uses the words "created" in this context, this means they were first. The reason behind this is mysterious and ever-reaching. God blessed them to be fruitful and multiply and replenish the earth. Because we now know that the Sons of God were first created, it will make everything fall into place the way God intended. That was not always the case. There are a lot of things in the written word that are made to be vague or mysterious. If certain things had been known earlier—1,000 years ago and leading up to this present day—it would have shed light on certain things that should not be revealed until now. Everything has to be in God's perfect timing.

The placement of everything by God, from the plant life to the trees with seed in them to the Sons of God, made it all possible. When God created the trees and vegetation, seed-bearing plants, and land-bearing fruit trees with seed in them, this was very important. All these things are for human consumption. They were not planted everywhere, only in certain areas and regions of the earth that would have regulated where the Sons of God lived. This has greater meaning, and I will explain in detail in the coming chapters.

Chapter 4

WHEN THE SONS of God started to replenish the Earth and subdue it, you may ask yourself: when did sin start on the Earth, and why? Sin would have happened naturally. You can picture it in your mind: two people walking along, and the person next to you trips and falls down. Your first reaction might be concern, and then your natural reaction, because of free will, might be a little laugh or snicker. You know we've all done it. The first time a person stepped on a stone or got a splinter, your natural reaction might not have been feeling pain in that moment. A natural reaction of our own free will may have caused you to say something stupid or maybe even some type of curse word.

We believe this is how sin would have started and continued. Today, there are a lot of natural human emotions: laughter, crying, pain, suffering, heartache, joy, and many others. That is why God allows for the forgiveness of sin, and I'm sure glad He does. Free will works both ways—sometimes for the good, and sometimes it turns out to be bad. Everyone, you have to keep in mind all this is in the beginning, but over time, through natural causes, the Sons of God found out that sin could give a certain power and advantage over others.

For thousands and thousands of years, even millions of years, the allure of sin started small. As sin grows, which it usually does, the progression of that will eventually rot and indicate society. The advantage of sin became apparent, and with sin creeping in, the nicest of sins started to subside. As we know, the wages of sin is death. But there were those among the Sons of God who distinguished themselves lived their lives in a righteous way. They loved their fellow man, worshiping God and praising Him, walking with Him all the days of their lives.

With the creation of life comes the reality of death because of the wages of sin. Eventually, the glorious way the Sons of God were created now becomes light. When the Sons of God started passing away from old age, sickness, or any other means of death, in those days, immediately after death, they received their celestial bodies and went to be with God in heaven. Because they were created in this amazing way, the Sons of God did not return to the Earth as modern man does when he dies. The spirit-body unity was created this way, and this is how we have gotten some of our angels, and they are still with us today.

They are ministering spirits sent by God to watch over His people. If you really think about it, what would make the best angel? It would be living their lives as the Sons of God first, knowing the hardships of love, the joy, the pain, and heartbreak, and the devotion of being a human first. This would give you the best perspective and insight. Knowing the people you were watching out for once were yourself. We know all about the stories written about God's wonderful angels in the written word of God with great power and great responsibility. Given free will by God, He does not have to micromanage every aspect of their lives. Our angels have the ability to react at a moment's notice to every situation that comes their way. This is no small feat.

The gravity of all of this is amazing, but with the freedom of free will, some will do wrong. And I believe you know where I'm going next.

Chapter 5

*Y*OU CAN BE certain that there were many Sons of God who stood out in their day-to-day lives here on Earth, like Michael. I'm sure there were many others who represented themselves in a pleasing way to God. We know that Michael when he got to heaven, became the archangel, a great and powerful angel, and the first angel. With the passing of time, our great and glorious heaven was filling up with celestial bodies. But as we know, trouble was on the horizon. Over time, Satan was stirring up trouble in heaven. His jealousy towards God was about to rear its ugly head, for we know that jealousy is one of the most destructive things on the planet and in heaven.

A war broke out in heaven. Michael and his angels fought against the dragon, and the dragon and his angels did not prevail; neither was their place found anymore in heaven. That great dragon was cast out, that old serpent called the devil and Satan. He was hurled to the Earth, and his angels were cast out with him. At this point in time, this is when evil would have started on Earth and still continues today. If you read Revelation chapter 12, verses 7 through 12, this explains what happened thousands of years ago:

"And there was war in heaven: Michael and his angels fought against the dragon, and the dragon fought and his angels, and prevailed not; neither was their place found anymore in heaven. And the great dragon was cast out, that old serpent, called the Devil, and Satan, which deceiveth the whole world: he was cast out into the Earth, and his angels were cast out with him. And I heard a loud voice saying in heaven, 'Now is come salvation, and strength, and the kingdom of our God, and the power of his Christ: for the accuser of our brethren is cast down, which accused them before our God day and night.'"

Salvation and strength mean rescue and safety, and the power of Christ—God's Son in heaven, not yet born—this means the Holy Spirit. His Christ, not our Christ. Satan and his angels are overcome by the blood of the Lamb, his Christ, and by the word of their testimony. "Rejoice, heavens, and ye that dwell in them. Woe to the inhabitants of the Earth and the sea! For the devil has come down to you, having great wrath, because he knows that he has but a short time."

The proper placement and thought in the mindset of scripture is so critical. You must stay in the confines of scripture. Scripture is God-breathed. There are no filler words in the Bible. Every word has meaning and proper context. Scripture must be tested with scripture.

Chapter 6

THE WORD OF God is absolute, whether we like it or not. If you are headed in the right direction as a believer, times and dates will not concern you. But if you are the evil one, the one hurled to the Earth, times and dates are everything. Before the scriptures were written, Satan had to take a very measured approach to everything. Not knowing the future without forethought, he knew this would be difficult. He has to make sure not to do too much too fast because he could accelerate his demise.

I want everyone to understand that I do not like talking about him in any way, shape, or form. After Satan and his angels were cast out into the Earth, this became his base of operation. His goal is to deceive the whole Earth. To achieve that, he will use a measured approach to everything. Because Satan was once human—one of the Sons of God—he knows all the ups and downs of being human. He also knows what it is to be an angel. Satan's approach to the pre-Adamic world in regard to technology was slow in nature. A little bit here and there would ensure his dominance, power, and manipulation over the pre-race of people.

Having lived as both a human and an angel, Satan and his angels will use that to their advantage. After their not-so-glorious departure from heaven, they were cast out into the Earth, and that was by design—out of sight, out of mind. By keeping their world hidden from mankind, the grand mystery of the Bible goes hand-in-hand. That's why having the proper understanding of everything from the beginning and in proper context allows you to start putting the pieces of the puzzle together. Before the Bible and the scriptures were written, they possibly had hundreds of thousands of years, and time was on their side for a long time.

They have set up shop in the bowels of the Earth. Because of their evil bent towards God and man for being hurled there, their motives are evil. They are all revolters, slanderers, brass, and iron—they are all corrupters. "The bellows are burned, the lead is consumed by the fire, the founder melts in vain, for the wicked are not plucked away. Reprobate silver shall men call them because the

Lord has rejected them." They are going to use man and technology to forward their evil agenda. None of this is very far-fetched if you look at it in a rational way.

Think about technology. Here in the United States, we have only been a country for a few hundred years. If you would add just say, 10,000 years to our technology, it would be mind-blowing. Let's just say they had a head start and know how to use that. The pre-Adamic world, in large part, wished to remain hidden. There are things being revealed now to explain words and proper context. When people take words out of context and put their own spin on them, that is very dangerous.

There is a narrative that has to do with the giants. They are mentioned in the Old Testament 12 times, but they are only mentioned once in this context. In Genesis chapter 6, verse 4, it states: "There were giants in the earth in those days, and also after that." This reference, and only this reference in this context, is talking about the fallen angels, the ones hurled to the Earth. They are evil. There are 11 other references to giants. Numbers states, "There were giants in the Earth in those days, and also after that." That means before the flood and after the flood.

Chapter 7

$\mathcal{I}$F YOU LOOK up the word "Giants" in Hebrew, it has many meanings, and none of them are very good. If you were to describe something evil, these are the words you would use: underneath, wither, below, tyrant, inferior position, condition, covertly, moderately, judged, accepted, cast down, divide away, fell, fugitive, overthrow, surely thrown down, bully, rot, slay, smite out. All of these terms describe the Giants—the ones hurled down. Most modern Bible translations use the word "Nephilim" instead of "Giants" or "celestial Giants," referring to the fallen angels mentioned in Genesis chapter 6, verse 4. There are also human-like giants, the Anakim and Rephaim, mentioned in the Old Testament.

Everything has to be looked at in its proper context. The giants mentioned in Numbers, Deuteronomy, and Joshua are all giants of human origin, not celestial. All the mysterious and vague ways are to keep mankind focused on God and what is good, not on the evil one or the fallen angel giants. They are mentioned in the most vile way without using curse words. We know they were created; they were the Sons of God with their celestial bodies because they are spirit-breathed, not formed from the Earth like Adam.

The ones who worship God immediately after death are caught up to heaven, or some become the angels that are with us today. But the ones who did not worship God, who were evil, are thrown into hell or gloomy dungeons. Since they are now celestial beings, they are held that way over possibly even millions of years. Satan's manipulation corrupted the pre-Adamic race of people, the men and women of the ancient world, and all the great beasts of the Earth. At this point in time, they were all corrupt, and every thought was continually evil. God knew that He was going to wipe mankind and all of the animals from the face of the Earth. God's patience with early man was slowly coming to an end.

I used to think, like many of you, that the world started with humanity with Adam at first. We now know that the world before Adam could be billions of years old. The understanding of the pre-Adamic world helps to put into context the timeline and the events that led to the creation story as we know it. The existence of giants and fallen angels plays a significant role in the narrative of corruption and redemption. Recognizing their influence and the subsequent actions of God helps us grasp the grand design and the ongoing battle between good and evil.

Understanding the true nature of these giants and the fallen angels sheds light on the broader context of the Bible. It reveals the layers of spiritual warfare and the lengths to which God goes to protect His creation and bring about His divine plan. This knowledge compels us to remain vigilant, focused on God, and aware of the forces that seek to lead us astray.

As we continue to explore these mysteries, let us keep our hearts and minds open to the teachings of the scripture. By doing so, we strengthen our faith and our understanding of the divine truths that guide our lives.

Chapter 8

WITH THE SHAPE and look of our Earth and the fossil records of all the great dinosaurs, the pre-Adamic world is undeniable. When Adam was formed by the Lord God, there was a different nature of God and a different nature of man. When Adam was formed, there was no mention of them. Remember, the Sons of God were created; Adam was formed. The Lord God formed Adam first. Adam was not created; he was formed by the Lord God out of the dust of the Earth. The deep and profound way Adam was formed is vastly different from the Sons of God. We know that the Sons of God were spirit-body unity, whereas Adam is a body-soul unity formed from the dust of the ground.

When the Lord God made the heavens (plural) and the Earth, this was for Adam's lineage. The forward creation of man was brought from the dust of the ground. From the creation of this earthly man, Adam, going forward is when you have more than one level of heaven, a different nature of man, and different levels of heaven. The Earth and the heaven created by the Lord God were to bring forth, advance, fulfill, or fashion a different nature of man, a different type of animals, and multiple levels of heaven. All this was created specially for the lineage of Adam.

The switch in the nature of God has profound meaning and consequences. When Adam and all his offspring going forward began, the fossil record with men started. It also means the way the Sons of God lived and breathed would be coming to an end. It also means the number of angels the Lord God needed at that point in time. The number of angels could be thousands upon thousands, $10,000 \times 10,000$, but the number of fallen angels is a mystery. I do not believe there are many. There are those in the church who believe that one-third were cast out of heaven, but even if the number is one-third, is it one-third of 10, one-third of 20, or one-third of 100? I do not believe it was a very large number.

Not having a large number, the devil and his angels have to be more sneaky, creative, manipulative, and downright evil to achieve world dominion. They cannot do it by walking everywhere. More on this a little later—you probably know where I'm going with the creation of Adam.

With the creation of Adam, the way things were done stopped. And the size of Satan's army stopped also. We know the end of the Sons of God's reign. Everyone on the planet at this point in time was corrupt, and every thought was evil. All this will play a huge part in the making of the Garden of Eden and the forming of Adam.

The giants are few in number, but the coffers of hell are many. Since they are celestial beings in gloomy dungeons, they will become Satan's little worker bees and his celestial army. But don't be confused about actual angels who sin and do wrong—they are held in gloomy dungeons also, but they are kept in everlasting chains. They are not accessible until the end.

With the looming flood and the not-so-distant future rapid expansion of hell for the Sons of God and the growth of Satan's evil warriors, the pre-Adamic world and all its corruption will soon come to an end. The breadth and scope of the pre-Adamic age, possibly billions of years old, and the reason behind it is amazing. But in large part, the world was to remain hidden.

Chapter 9

$\mathcal{T}$HE ANCIENT WORLD of the first created beings, from the great creatures of the sea to the great beasts of the Earth, birds of the air, and the first created human beings, would have been an amazing and wonderful sight to see. But that world became so corrupted, rotten, and evil that God wanted it to remain hidden. The pre-world sheds light on many things that we now know are bad. The placement by God in the beginning, from plant life to everything with seed in it, was meant to keep that hidden.

In the time before Adam, there was no shrub or plant in the field that had sprung up. This is the first time "field" is mentioned—it was in Genesis 2 when the Lord God made the Earth and Heavens. The Earth and Heavens made by the Lord God were to bring forth, advance, fulfill, or fashion a different nature of man, different types of animals, and multiple levels of heaven created specifically for the lineage of Adam. If you use the proper meaning of the scriptures, from the Sons of God to the giants, to Adam and then Eve, and through to Noah, it all makes perfect sense.

After the Lord God made the Earth and Heavens, you can look up the word "made" in Hebrew. It has many meanings: accomplish, advance, appoint, bear, bestow, bring forth, dress, execute, fashion, fulfill, furnish, gather, finish, or govern. You can pick some of these applications for the reason and meaning behind the making and forming of Adam. The creation of the Heavens and the Earth had already been done. The shift in the nature of God and the way things are done now is profound. The Lord God is not done with us yet, or none of us would be here.

The Sons of God were hunters, not farmers. Adam was formed by the Lord God to bring forth a new creation of men to populate the Earth. The men and women of the ancient world were all corrupt, and every thought was evil continually. The Lord God knew He was going to destroy the whole planet with a great flood. Because of God's forethought, knowing the beginning to the end, you will soon understand the gravity of the placement of everything—from man to beast to trees with seed in them.

In the beginning, you had the spirit of God's first creation—the ancient world—and you had the making of the Earth and the Heavens and the Garden of Eden by the Lord. These were two separate places, old and new. They were different natures of God, different kinds of creatures. You had a different kind of man in the sense of how he was formed, not created. The Lord God took a hands-on approach. The Lord God breathed, planted, and walked. The shift from God to the Lord God is a clear separation. The Sons of God were spoken into being, while Adam was formed out of the dust of the Earth—completely different, but they are both flesh. I will explain later how profound that is.

In the macro sense of the word of God, it is so complex and amazing, yet so mysterious, that you have to look at every word, no matter how small, in proper context. The meat of the word is not for the faint of heart, but if you look at the milk of the word with what you know, you can see how everything is starting to fall into place. All the new creatures created for the fields and the Garden of Eden and that remain in that region of the Earth, will be in the line and lineage of what you see with Adam and Eve going forward.

From the Garden of Eden to the new creatures of the Earth to the fields—all of the work of the Lord God with Adam going forward—since the creating has been done, this is a continuance. That is why the Lord God used the word "made" the Earth and the Heavens. Every word has to be looked at in the proper context. You may be wondering why the world could have gone on and thrived for billions of years. The Sons of God were able to live their lives without evil in it. In everyday circumstances, sin and death without evil could survive for billions of years, and it did.

When the devil and his angels were hurled to the Earth, the corruption, manipulation, and perversion slowly began. The devil had measured all of his schemes, knowing he angered God. Without forethought and not having a crystal ball for the future, he did not want to do too much too fast. He is not God.

Chapter 10

IN THE BEGINNING, we have the Spirit of God and His grand and glorious creation. The fossil record of all the dinosaurs and all the great beasts of the Earth would have been amazing. A world without evil in it was able to flourish. This creation, the pre-Adamic world, was in large part meant to remain hidden. I will explain a little later on how important that is.

The Lord God said, "It is not good for man to be alone." The Lord God could not find a suitable helper for Adam. There was no suitable helper because all the Sons of God at this point in time were corrupt, and every thought was evil. If you are in the camp where the pre-Adamic world didn't exist, why would God be looking for a suitable helper if Adam was the only person on Earth? It doesn't make sense; it's probably not true. The first created beings were all corrupt. Having the understanding of scripture now, it is becoming clear. Always keep in mind that the Bible is a mystery.

The Lord God caused Adam to fall into a deep sleep. The Lord God took one of the man's ribs and closed the place with flesh. The Lord God made a woman from the rib He had taken out of Adam. She will be called Woman. The Garden of Eden and that region of the Earth would have been different because all of the creatures in this region were different—not compatible with the dinosaurs and the great beasts of the first created beings. They would not have been able to wander too far from their food source. They probably required a more tropical climate. There was no rain on the Earth in those days, so everything would have been located around some type of water source. You have to know the world in those days was connected, meaning the landmasses would have been enormous.

When the Lord God made the Garden of Eden and the fields, this area would have been separate. The Lord caused a mist to come up and water the face of the ground, with no rain anywhere else. This vast region would flourish. Before the temptation of Adam and Eve, there was no hostility between them. Everything would have been peachy; there was no strife. After the fall, when Adam and

Eve were in the Garden of Eden, the Lord God put enmity between them and their offspring. They would have looked different after they were banned from the Garden of Eden.

The nature of God shifts again to the Lord. When the Lord put enmity between Adam and Eve and their offspring, their sons and daughters would have looked at each other in a different way. Instead of seeing each other as brother and sister and feeling that closeness, it would have been like seeing a man or a woman—they were related, but it didn't feel as if they were. After their eyes were opened to know good and evil, the ambiguity between a husband and wife, son and daughter, brother and sister would have changed. The mindset would not feel perverted. Before, that bond and closeness, being naked and feeling no shame with each other, would have been amazing. Because of sin and the shame that comes along with it, the Lord put that enmity in so things would not seem perverted.

Everyone has thought about their offspring, their children, brothers, or sisters having children. To us, it seems weird. When God puts a word in the Bible like "enmity" and every other phrase that is in the word of God, you take the words very carefully. This is why understanding the deeper meanings behind these words is essential. The shift in relationships and perceptions after the fall was necessary to prevent further corruption and to set the foundation for humanity's new path.

As we continue to delve into the scriptures, we see the intricate plan of God unfolding. Each word, each phrase carefully chosen, reveals the profound truths that guide us. The shift from the pre-Adamic world to the creation of Adam and Eve marks a pivotal point in the grand design, setting the stage for the redemption and salvation that would come through God's continued work with humanity.

Chapter 11

$\mathcal{I}$N GENESIS 4, when Adam knew his wife, Eve, she became pregnant. It mentions his wife's name directly because there was no ambiguity between Adam and Eve. Like most people reading about Adam and Eve and all the details, it is very mysterious and confusing— that was by design. The pre-Adamic world, in regards to the first created beings and, in large part, the fallen angels, was to remain hidden. More on the subject a little later on.

When Eve gave birth with the help of the Lord, everything at this point was done with the Lord's blessing. She gave birth to Cain. We know that the Sons of God at this juncture were all evil, so any interactions between Adam, Eve, and Cain with the Sons of God would have been suspect. After Cain killed Abel, the Lord said, "You are driven from the area. You will be a restless wanderer on the Earth." Cain said, "But whoever finds me will kill me."

But the Lord said, "Not so; if anyone kills Cain, he will suffer vengeance seven times over." The Lord put a mark on Cain so that whoever found him would not kill him. This could have been literal or figurative—a signal, a flag, a beacon, a monument, an open mark, or a sign, a token.

So Cain went out of the Lord's presence and lived in the land of Nod, which meant "to wander." Cain traveled east of Eden. Cain probably followed the river to the east, towards Syria or that region. He could have ended up in Beth-Eden, a place of pleasure. Just picture a young man, probably not schooled, naïve, and an easy target for manipulation. Being under a curse himself, none of this would have the blessings of the Lord because the world at this time was filled with violence. Anyone he encountered would have been evil.

It states in Genesis 4 that Cain knew his wife, and she became pregnant. If you look at the word "knew," it has several meanings: to know, to be known, be aware, acknowledge, recognition, declare, observe, and other meanings. Just because Cain knew his wife was pregnant doesn't mean it was his child. All this hanky-panky going on lets you know that Cain's wife was pregnant but from someone other than Cain because it does not mention her name. There is no direct cause to be certain she was his.

I'm sure she told Cain it was his son. He thought, at this time, he had two sons. If Cain knew it was someone else's child, he would not have named a city after him.

Once again, the ancient world was vast and perverted and would soon come to an end. Why would the Lord put a mark on Cain if there was no one else on the planet? Adam and Eve knew who he was. Cain was driven from the ground where he grew up and headed for unfamiliar territory. Having that mark on him was the only thing that saved him for a time. Cain was cursed; he would have become a fugitive and a vagabond. "From the face of the Earth and from Thy face shall I be hid." You have to understand the gravity of all of this.

All the interactions that Cain would have had and did have would have been with the Sons of God. It was like Sodom and Gomorrah on steroids. There would have been no access to Cain or any of their progeny. So, everything points to a vast world of corrupt and perverted people at the end of their reign. I've told you that the Sons of God, being the pre-Adamic race of people and all their ilk, were to remain hidden. In due time, I will be tying all of this together. Because of God's forethought and His divine wisdom, you will understand why it was done that way.

Chapter 12

CAIN'S WIFE BORE Enoch, and Enoch fathered Irad. Irad fathered Mehujael, Mehujael fathered Methusael, and Methusael fathered Lamech. It's important to remember that at this time, Cain had no direct causation with his sons, but he did not know that. Lamech married two women, one named Adah and the other Zillah. Adah gave birth to Jabal, who was the father of those who lived in tents and raised livestock. His brother's name was Jubal, and he was the father of all who played the harp and flute. Zillah also had a son, Tubal-Cain, who forged all kinds of tools out of bronze and iron. Tubal-Cain's sister was Naamah.

There is a lot of information here. All of this technology was very rudimentary for the amount of time the Sons of God were on Earth. When I told you earlier in the book that when the devil and his angels were hurled to Earth, he had to be very measured in all his evil schemes. His manipulation with the use of technology will serve him well. All these technological advances came from the ancient world, from Satan. At this time, they were raising livestock because they were eating meat, another perversion they were not supposed to do. But at this point, nothing was off-limits.

The advancement of technology happened too fast—it could have jeopardized his evil plot. Satan would give a little information and technology here and there. Like I said before, he does not have the ability of forethought like God, and at this time, he does not have the written word of God yet. He is like a drug dealer, giving a little bit here and there, getting you hooked so you keep coming back for more. Wouldn't you want to be the first person to build a fire, make a tent for shelter, play and make a musical instrument, or domesticate cattle? All these little tidbits of information would make someone very popular in the community. It could make them very important and powerful. They became mighty men of old, men of renown.

There is no stretch of the imagination that the devil and his angels, at this juncture, had a vast and superior technological advantage, being around for thousands and

Rick Nehrt

thousands of years. You can see how that would be possible. Can you imagine back then if you were off by yourself and someone rode by you on a bike? That would be amazing to see in your life. It could also make you more powerful. Satan will distract and take your eyes off God's grand and glorious creation by manipulation and making everything God created dark and ugly, and that is what he did and is still doing.

Over time, the ancient world, along with the Sons of God, their society, and their way of life, became so dark and ugly. They evolved because of sin and evil. Even the greatest dinosaurs were eating meat; humans were eating meat, and all this perversion blurred every descent line. The making by the Lord God of the Earth and heaven for Adam and his lineage going forward was to stop the rot and decay of the first created. It was slowly creeping into their society, starting with Cain.

Lamech married Adah and Zillah. Zillah had a son named Tubal-Cain. When they used Tubal's last name, that was very specific. This means Zillah committed adultery with Cain. This is the first time that the Sons of God and the children of men (Adam's lineage) would have intersected with the birth of Tubal-Cain. Lamech was mad, so he killed Cain and also killed Tubal-Cain, Cain's son.

All this perversion and adultery going on was not what the Lord wanted—the Sons of God mingling with the children of men at this time.

The first created were all evil. There were many things going on in the world with many people, and none of it was good. Adam knew his wife again, and she bore a son and called his name Seth. When it was said Adam knew his wife again, it did not mention her as his wife. I'm sure that Adam and Eve had many children, and their children had children, and so on and so forth over many years. Adam's wife had a son, for God said He has appointed me another seed instead of Abel, whom Cain slew. The seed of Seth was crucial.

Adam lived 130 years and begot a son in his own likeness, after his image, and called his name Seth. He was far enough down the line, separate from Eve, so he took on the characteristics of Adam. This is the direct line going forward that the Lord wanted. From Seth to Enos, then began men to call upon the Lord. The direct line from Seth to Enos, all the way to Noah, remained righteous and true.

Chapter 13

MAN'S WICKEDNESS ON Earth had corrupted his way. "The end of all flesh has come before me, for the Earth is filled with violence through them, and behold, I will destroy them with the Earth." When the Lord said "them," this means, in context, mankind: the Sons of God and men in Adam's indirect line. In Chapter 6 of Genesis, men began to multiply on the face of the Earth—this is Adam's lineage—and daughters were born to them. The Sons of God saw that the daughters of men were fair and took them as wives of all that they chose.

Remember the making of the Earth and the heavens by the Lord God, and the Garden of Eden, and the forming of Adam and his lineage going forward is what the Lord wanted. When the Sons of God came unto the daughters of men, and they bore children, the same became men of old, men of renown. Some became powerful tyrants and giants, very tall, and none righteous. At this time, all men except Adam's direct line were wicked. The Lord said, "My spirit shall not always strive with man, for that he is also flesh. His days shall be 120 years."

Every word in the Bible is important, and it is important for a reason. When it states "flesh," this means that the Sons of God and the children of men, their children, would be flesh. The children became mighty men of renown. The combination of the two—still flesh—had a different DNA structure. The Sons of God are spirit-breathed human bodies, not formed from the Earth. They were spoken into existence. Adam was formed from the dust of the ground. The Sons of God were spirit. When they die, there is no fossil record of them. The fossil record started with Adam and Eve because they were formed, not created. But when the Sons of God came unto the daughters of men, there might be a fossil record of them.

The name Adam can be used in many ways. In Genesis, "This is the book of the generations of Adam. In the day that God created man, in the likeness of God made He him. Male and female created He them, and blessed them, and called their name Adam in the day when they were created." In this context, the name Adam is being used to refer to the first created male and female by God.

The corruption of mankind had reached a tipping point. The blending of the Sons of God with the daughters of men created a race of giants and men of renown who were powerful but morally corrupt. The wickedness that spread throughout the Earth was unparalleled. The Lord's declaration that His spirit would not strive with man forever and that man's days would be limited to 120 years marked the beginning of the end of this corrupt era.

The interaction between the Sons of God and the daughters of men resulted in a hybrid race that still possessed flesh. This distinction is crucial, as it highlights the difference between the original spiritual nature of the Sons of God and the earthly nature of Adam's descendants. This hybridization introduced a new level of depravity and wickedness that warranted divine intervention.

The fossil record, beginning with Adam and Eve, indicates the transition from purely spiritual beings to those formed from the dust of the ground. The hybrid offspring of the Sons of God and the daughters of men may have left a fossil record, bridging the gap between the ancient, pre-Adamic world and the post-Adamic era.

As we continue to unravel the mysteries of Genesis, we see the consequences of straying from God's intended path. The intermingling of the divine with the earthly led to unprecedented corruption and violence, necessitating a reset in the form of the Great Flood. The narrative underscores the importance of adhering to God's plan and the dire consequences of deviation.

In the broader context of the Bible, the story of the Sons of God and the daughters of men serves as a cautionary tale. It reminds us of the delicate balance between the spiritual and the earthly and the need to maintain our focus on God's will. The preservation of Adam's direct lineage through Seth and Enos, leading to Noah, signifies the hope and continuity of God's promise amidst the chaos and corruption of the ancient world.

Chapter 14

FOR HUNDREDS OF years, archaeologists have been digging up old structures of the ancient world. I believe many of these structures are thousands of years older than originally dated. The pre-Adamic world in the beginning would have been amazing—a world before evil reared its ugly head. With all the great beasts of the Earth, man and beast were no threat to each other because, in the beginning, both were vegetarians. There was no rain on the Earth in those days, and the dwellings and structures of the Sons of God would have been simple and rudimentary. There would have been no need for elaborate structures; the climate was very temperate.

After the devil and his angels were hurled to the Earth, everything changed. Because of the design and forethought by God, the first created humans, the world could be covered up with a great flood. The elusive fossil remains of early man have puzzled archaeologists, and rightly so. There is no fossil record of early man, but you would find structures they created buried beneath the ancient buildings. You might find footprints of the Sons of God, but no fossil remains—footprints may have already been found.

The placement of everything in the beginning—all the plant life with the seed in it, the fruit trees, and other trees with the seed in them—was perfect. This placement would regulate growth and rejuvenate the Earth after the flood. Because of the design of everything good by God, it was allowed that the church did not adhere to a race of people—that was by design. There was no real harm in that; for thousands of years, it kept the focus off that mysterious world where so much good came from, but it also kept the focus off the giants, the ones in Genesis 4, the fallen angels.

It states that there were giants on the Earth in those days and also after that. This means before the flood and after the flood. You may think this is confusing, and it is. We know now that the giants mentioned in Genesis 6:4 are celestial beings—the fallen angels. They are not human. That is the only way they could have made it through the great flood to come; they did not have the breath of life in them. God put that in the mix of the mighty men who were of old, men of renown. Remember, it says "men of renown," not angels. This is paramount. The same became mighty men, human men. Some of the men were giants, and this was allowed to be misconstrued for thousands of years. It kept the focus off the fallen angels or celestial giants.

If the true nature of them had become mainstream with humanity years ago, all focus would have been on them. Satan would have loved that. God knows the curiosities of the human race, which is why things are mysterious in the word of God. It is to keep us on a righteous path and to focus on what is good, but it also keeps the devil and his angels guessing. Before the written word, Satan did not have the ability to look into the future. That is why he's been very measured about his schemes.

Everything we need to know about the past and all the way to the future is in the word of God. Times and dates are known to God only. Keeping the focus off the giants was paramount. Before the flood, the road from Adam to Noah would have been chaotic if it were out of place in the word of God. The world would have seen chaos like never before.

I'm going to explain to you how important the wording and timing is. There are certain people in the Bible, like Enoch, who walked with God for over 300 years, and then he was no more, for God took him away. When he walked with God, that was no small statement. His writings would have put a focus on mysterious things that should not have been revealed until now. The mystery of the word of God is so amazing. Everything from the beginning to the end is in the written word. Once you understand why it was written this way, the puzzle pieces come together.

I'm going to give you a scenario of why the word was done in this manner. Let's just say, for argument's sake, that because Enoch walked with God, he was being targeted by aliens—the fallen angels—taken in a spacecraft to show how superior their technology is. The world would not be ready for that. It would have put a focus on supernatural beings and pure evil at a time when the world was not ready for it. I cannot put into words how important that is. That is why the word of God is a mystery. The word of God is never changing; it is righteous and true, with no need for updates. The manner in which every word was written, with perfect placement, timing, and context at certain places in time for all humanity, makes it clear that it is divine.

Chapter 15

BEFORE THE FLOOD, the Sons of God were marrying the daughters of men. The Lord said, "My spirit will not contend with man forever, for he is mortal." Remember, He did not say to contend with angels forever. Man first, man—the Sons of God—for he is mortal. He did not say, "for he is celestial." This is a clear distinction. There are books, TV programs, and shows on Christian networks about humans having sex with angels. Some of these narratives come from certain interpretations within the church. However, God's word will not be perverted.

These interpretations arise because some do not believe that the Sons of God were the first created. These mixed messages from some in the church community, along with many other deceptive teachings, have almost destroyed the whole planet. Some fallacies have been taught for so long that they are taken as gospel. Some of the things I will discuss later in this book may not sit well with many in the church community. The church cannot continue on the path it is on. God is growing angry with His people, and we are running out of time. Whether you are on the side of good or on the side of evil, time is running out.

Certain doctrines that have become mainstream in the church have led to complacency, which runs deep. The idea of angels having sex with humans, among other statements, causes confusion. Angels are celestial beings; they are not human. They are ministering spirits. As stated in Hebrews 1:5, "For to which of the angels did God ever say, 'You are my Son; today I have become your Father'?" Angels are not taken in marriage. This stands true for fallen angels as well. God's angels and Satan's angels are still celestial beings.

On the side of good and another on the side of evil, the Lord saw how wickedness on Earth had become and that every inclination of the thoughts of man's heart was evil all the time. The Lord was grieved that He had made man on the Earth, and His heart was filled with pain. So the Lord said, "I will wipe mankind, whom I created, from the face of the Earth—men and animals, and creatures that move along the ground, and birds of the air—for I am grieved that I have made them." But Noah found favor in the eyes of the Lord.

Noah, his wife, his family—Shem, Ham, and Japheth—and their wives were saved. After Noah built the ark, God commanded him to take with him seven of every kind of clean animal, a male, and its mate, and seven of every kind of bird, male and female, to keep various kinds alive throughout the Earth. Two of every living creature, male and female, were also to be taken on the ark. The waters prevailed exceedingly, covering the Earth by 20 feet above the tallest peak. All in whose nostrils was the breath of life, and all that was on dry land died. Every living substance was destroyed, both man and cattle, and the creeping things, and the fowls of heaven. Only Noah and those with him in the ark remained alive.

After the flood, God told them to be fruitful and increase in number, multiply on the Earth, and increase upon it. Because of God's forethought, the placement of seed and fruit trees and other trees with seed in them would rejuvenate the Earth after the flood. When the waters receded, the mud would have covered most places, burying much of the ancient world. The trees and life with seed in them would have sprouted and grown in the places where they were before. After the flood, when areas became populated, many structures would have been built over the ancient ones. This design kept the ancient world buried beneath the mud, allowing a new world to flourish above, keeping the pre-Adamic world and the Sons of God a mystery until the proper time.

God said, "All life under the heavens, every creature, all flesh that has the breath of life in it, will perish; all mankind." The giants vaguely mentioned in Genesis 6:4 made it past the flood. They were there in those days and also after that because they are the fallen angels, celestial beings. They do not breathe air; they do not have the breath of life in them. That is how they made it through the great flood of God. They were the first created humans, and their existence has remained a mystery, as intended.

Chapter 16

$\mathcal{N}$OW THAT YOU understand who the fallen angels are, and you understand how Adam and Eve were formed, not created, and when the Sons of God came unto the daughters of men and had children by them, you can make sense of it all. I hope you see how important the word of God is. The words chosen by God and their proper placement and timing are paramount.

Let's consider another scenario in Genesis 6:4. If you substitute the word "Giants" for the word "extraterrestrials," even at that time, the meaning would have been clear. Or, use the word "fallen angels" in place of "Giants." Nothing else would have mattered because of man's curiosity about anything outside the norm of society. One word out of place would have disrupted the whole planet. God chose the perfect words at the perfect time and place.

Because we have God's written word and we can see His grand and glorious creation, there are no excuses. Society at large is breaking down—you can see it and feel it. This was no accident. After the written word, the devil and his angels scrutinized every word. They know every word is true. When the Old Testament talked about the Messiah, it set off alarms in their heads. This was something tangible they could see. Before the written word, they had to be very measured. Having been on the Earth for thousands of years, scheming, lying, and manipulating mankind, and setting up their eventual demise, they were always looking for a heads-up.

When Christ was born through the Virgin Mary, this was one of the prophetic triggers that let them know they were on a downhill slide. Just think of the gravity of all this—being in the bowels of the Earth for thousands and thousands of years, acquiring superior technology like the world has never seen. Throughout history, with the subtle use of technology, Satan has created all sorts of religions. They could target one person in an indigenous tribe and give him a little advanced knowledge to make him stand out above the rest of the tribe so he would be revered and worshiped. You can see how the subtle manipulation of technology could shape the world in an evil way, and this is still being done today.

Throughout time, over thousands of years, this explains why we have so many religions spread out across the planet. Satan could manipulate people by walking up and handing them a "bible" of sorts or an important document, making that person stand out. That person would be revered and worshiped. All the different religions and different technologies serve as distractions. You have to remember the devil and his angels do not care who you worship as long as you do not worship God. You can pray to any god you want—you can worship a frog, a stick, a rock, a snake—and Satan will give you the tools to do that, as long as you don't worship the God of heaven, their Creator.

Everyone is looking to the stars and the planets and what is out in space for answers. A fortress of solitude, the North Country, a hidden world, dark and gloomy, a place of covering over a secret place, a place to look on or lay up. They are all corrupters. "The bellows are burned, the lead is consumed by the fire, the founder melts in vain, for the wicked are not plucked away. Reprobate silver shall men call them because the Lord has rejected them." Everything they need is right under their feet.

Chapter 17

KNOWING WHAT YOU know now, and understanding how everything started and the reasoning behind the way things were worded for a never-changing Bible in an ever-changing world, timing is everything. Just think about it: where would the best place for Satan to set up shop be? On some desolate planet somewhere with few resources, or in our Earth, with a plethora of minerals, iron, metals, gold, silver, and every metal known to man right under our feet?

They have been in our Earth for thousands and thousands of years, lounging around in its security. There is no stretch of the imagination required to see what the world would look like with their advanced technology. Always keep in mind what they are: they are evil. It is awful and terrifying beyond words, but it is true and relevant to our time in history when they will finally be revealed in grand fashion or gradually by governments, television programs, and other forms of media. The devil wants to be given his due.

With the way the world is now, and what is on TV, on phones, computers, even cartoons—every kind of weirdness your mind can imagine is out there, desensitizing the whole world to their existence. If there was anything that should be shocking, it would be them. But in society, because we have been desensitized to their existence, it is no longer as shocking as it should be. Do not be fooled. Be very, very careful.

The statute of limitations has run out after the birth of our Christ. It has been several thousand years since then, which may seem like a long time, but the first prophetic trigger that raised the alarm was when they started scheming in heaven, and that did not go well for them. Satan is angry for being hurled down. In modern terminology, they are called aliens or extraterrestrials. They are evil and should not be sought after or looked upon. They should only be mentioned in the darkest of terms. Do not be fooled by cute pictures, cartoons, T-shirts, or television programs. Remember, Satan himself masquerades as an angel of light (2 Corinthians 11:14). He knows his time is short.

Around the time the Jewish people were trying to become a state, that set alarm bells off—a prophetic trigger like the world has never seen. When that was being debated, the devil and his angels said, "Oh, crap." The ramifications and prophetic meanings of what was taking place set things in motion that would change the world in the wrong direction in a relatively short amount of time. You may ask yourself, why now? The degeneration of our society is apparent. Satan has used technology in a very measured way, as I've said before, for thousands of years.

I do not know if I can put into words the desperation and shock that took place in Satan's evil kingdom when the Jews got their homeland back. They are running out of time, with a clock ticking. Now you can see it, and you can feel it. Just think about what took place. The devil and his angels—extraterrestrials—have been around for thousands of years, scheming and manipulating the world. If you knew in relatively short order that your days were numbered, knowing your fate and the fate of your whole kingdom would soon be coming to a tragic end, that's why things are ramping up.

Around the same period of time, Satan made some very bold moves. He caused some spacecraft in strategic places around the world to crash. The reported crashes around the world would ensure that nations would have to harvest their technology so another nation would not get the upper hand. Desperate times call for desperate measures, even knowing that the origins of what they found were evil.

In conclusion, the world we live in is under great influence by these fallen beings. They manipulate, deceive, and corrupt using technology and false ideologies. The narrative they spin is designed to distract humanity from the truth. This manipulation extends to creating religions, societal norms, and even political structures. The objective is simple: keep humanity from worshiping the one true God.

As believers, it is crucial to stay vigilant and grounded in the word of God. The Bible provides clarity and direction in these confusing times. Understanding the nature of these fallen beings and their schemes helps us to navigate the spiritual landscape with discernment. The urgency of our times calls for a deeper commitment to faith and a readiness to stand against the deceptions that pervade our world.

Chapter 18

I BELIEVE OUR GOVERNMENT knew they were the fallen angels—the ones hurled to the Earth as spoken about in Revelation 12—but at the time of the crash, they did not know that. The crash was a planned and evil plot that shocked everyone in the know. The technology was so advanced that it would take years to reverse engineer. This is how Satan has gotten a foothold on the nations around the world. Many nations and countries around the world are not what we would call Christian nations; I would say most are secular. Satan does not have to win them over, but the Christian nations of the world would need to be persuaded.

Technology has been used by Satan around the world since he was hurled to the Earth. I've stated this many times. Because they knew who they were, our government's secrecy was paramount for more than one reason.

They had to keep them secret. They had to do everything in their power to keep mankind from knowing the truth about extraterrestrials. They have tried to shield the world from their existence, especially our government of old and the governments of that era. They knew the ramifications if that information got out to the masses.

I believe our government of that era knew they were evil. Our government and other governments were in a precarious position at that time. They had no idea that they were being played—a sneaky and manipulative move driven by desperation because the biblical time clock for them was running out. For us as humans, 100 years seems like an eternity, but with God, a day is but 1,000 years, and 1,000 years is but a day. From Adam in the Garden of Eden going forward to where we are now, in the grand scheme of things, it's just a blip on the radar.

I've stated this before the Devil and his angels—extraterrestrials—have been around in some form or fashion for thousands of years. If you found out that your evil empire was running out of time, knowing that your fate is sealed, that is why the gloves are off. The spacecraft that crashed in strategic places and their occupants would have been shocking to anyone involved—something the world would not be ready for. I do not believe that the aliens were the fallen angelsThey were some genetically mutated beings created in their lab or some of their little worker bees from the gloomy dungeons. For fallen angels, I do not believe they were in the down craft.

I have stated this before, but it is worth mentioning again: after they were hurled to the Earth, I do not believe there was a large number of them. Satan has to try to keep the upper hand. To sacrifice any fallen angel is not an option. He would not want any perspective doing an autopsy on one of them, gaining knowledge and understanding of who they were and what their genetic makeup is. So, they put some outdated spacecraft and hurled them to the Earth.

You may think this is crazy and far out there, and you are right. Without knowledge and understanding, this would seem Greek to you. But because you have the true grasp of what took place in the beginning, with a spirit-breathed pre-Adamic race of humans millions of years before the Garden of Eden and all that followed, you can see how all this is possible. The spacecraft would have been so advanced, especially at that time. And after the shock wore off, they could not wait to get busy reverse-engineering what they recovered.

These reverse-engineered technologies have since infiltrated every aspect of modern society. Our governments, hungry for power and technological supremacy, have unwittingly played into the hands of these fallen beings. The rapid advancements in technology and the increasingly secular nature of societies worldwide are no coincidence. They are part of a grander scheme to divert humanity's attention away from God and towards the material and the temporal.

The secrecy surrounding these events, the manipulation of information, and the strategic dissemination of technology all serve to fulfill Satan's ultimate goal: to turn humanity away from God. The fallen angels, masquerading as extraterrestrials, are tools in this grand deception. They present themselves as advanced beings from other worlds, offering knowledge and technology, but their true nature and intentions are far more sinister.

As believers, it is imperative to stay vigilant and grounded in the word of God. The Bible provides us with the discernment needed to navigate these confusing and deceptive times. By understanding the true nature of these fallen beings and their schemes, we can resist their influence and remain faithful to God.

In the end, the truth will prevail. God's plan is unfolding, and no amount of deception or technological advancement can thwart His will. The fallen angels, their schemes, and their influence will be exposed and defeated.

Until that day, we must remain steadfast in our faith, discerning in our understanding, and unwavering in our commitment to God.

Chapter 19

PLAYING RIGHT INTO the devil's hands, I do not have any inside information on these topics; I am staying with the word of God. Everything I'm telling you is a rational way to look at what happened from a biblical perspective. Knowing the truth of how the universe started, how everything was created or made, and how the devil and his angels were hurled to the Earth and why that happened, it is no stretch of the imagination that this could all make sense. They are not from Mars or any other planet inside or outside our solar system. There were small groups of angels with free will, arguing, lying, and scheming in heaven, making trouble because of jealousy and trying to recruit more angels to follow them. After a war in heaven, in which they lost their place, God hurled them to Earth.

That's why Satan is enraged. Because of his advanced technology, eventually, they would need help reverse-engineering the spacecraft. To us, the spacecraft was so advanced that the kind of help they needed did not come from above; they would have to seek the devil and his angels for help. Seeking his help is what he wanted. Understand that even knowing the origins of where it came from was evil. The devil was sneaky because the spacecraft was an old, outdated craft that they came up with hundreds or thousands of years ago. You can see how that happened because of time. We've only been a country a few hundred years; they've been around for thousands.

I've stated this before, but it is becoming more relevant now. To them, the crashed spacecraft was like a bicycle—old and outdated technology. We had a flood and a rapid growth of technology in the last 50 or 60 years, and this has come with a price. The whole world is distracted; everyone is stuck on their phones or computers. Wake up! Be aware of what is going on around you. God is a very jealous God. The world is so distracted and so desensitized to all the weirdness going on in the world that nothing will shock them now.

Our government has done everything in its power to keep mankind from knowing the truth about extraterrestrials in modern-day terminology. They have shielded the world from their evil. I believe that was the right thing to do. They went to extreme measures to make that happen. One piece of the puzzle put in place at the wrong time, especially in the 40s and 50s, would have set things in motion that the world was not ready for yet. Keep in mind all of this was orchestrated by the devil because of the time restraints. Desperate times called for desperate measures. Our government did not know at the time they were being played. Time for the devil and his angels was something they had plenty of.

When the Jewish people got their homeland back, as I stated before, time for all is running out. A world so distracted and so focused on their devices that they cannot see what is going on right in front of them. There are things out there that go bump in the night. There are a very select few in our government who know what happened in the past regarding the fallen angels and what is going on today. We, as a nation, have fallen for the trap—the bait—just like in the past. The bait was technology.

Eventually, technology will reach the end of the road. We are humans, body-soul unity. We have limitations created by God to keep us guarded and grounded. Because of our limitations, the devil knows the technology spectrum with us as humans regarding reverse-engineering the downed spacecraft. Because we are not celestial beings, we humans cannot take the forces that were by design.

The devil's deception is multi-faceted. He uses technology as bait, knowing that humans, with our innate curiosity and desire for advancement, would latch onto it without hesitation. The rapid advancements in technology have brought about unprecedented changes in our society, but they have also brought about unprecedented distractions. We are more connected than ever before, yet more disconnected from the truth and from God.

The government's secrecy was an attempt to shield humanity from the harsh reality of these fallen beings. They knew the panic and chaos that would ensue if the truth were to be revealed. However, the devil and his angels are cunning. They have used this secrecy to their advantage, manipulating and controlling behind the scenes.

As believers, we must remain vigilant. We must not be swayed by the allure of technology or the distractions of this world. We must keep our focus on God and His word. The Bible is our guide, our source of truth, and our shield against the deceptions of the devil. The fallen angels may have advanced technology, but they do not have the power of God. They may have knowledge, but they do not have the wisdom of God.

In the end, God's truth will prevail. The deceptions of the devil will be exposed, and the true nature of these fallen beings will be revealed. Until that day, we must remain steadfast in our faith, grounded in the word of God, and vigilant against the distractions and deceptions of this world.

Chapter 20

I KNOW THIS ALL sounds crazy because it is crazy. The way things are with the world—all their distractions, everyone stuck in their devices, and all the mixed messages coming from the church—everything is playing right into the devil's hand. God is angry at the church; the church has let the world down. More on this later.

Our government has used extreme measures to keep mankind from knowing about extraterrestrials. I would have done the same thing. I hope our government did not make a deal with the devil. We are slowly being desensitized about their existence. Always keep in mind what they are, no matter what you see or hear of all the great things they have done or what they might do. Don't be fooled. Remember, "For our struggle is not against flesh and blood, but against the rulers, against the authorities, against the powers of this dark world, and against the spiritual forces of evil in the heavenly realms" (Ephesians 6:12). That's what we're up against.

Because of the downed spacecraft in strategic places across the globe, secrecy was paramount. The extreme measures taken by very few in the know in the beginning were probably justified. You hear of some of the extreme measures taken by some in our government. I hope you understand how shocking it would have been at that period of time for our government to deal with the downed spacecraft, knowing they were the fallen angels—or at least thinking they were the fallen angels. The origin of the craft was the product of the fallen angels, but the occupants were not the fallen angels—a sneaky move by the devil.

I do not believe that the devil knew our government would go to such extremes, and boy, did they go to extremes. The devil was probably banking on a quicker and more public response. This was not allowed by our government, especially in the 40s, 50s, and even the 60s. When JFK was president in the '60s, he believed a more transparent government was needed. There was talk that he was going to go public with the information about the downed spacecraft. That shocking revelation at that time could not be allowed.

I understand transparency, but the United States and other countries were not ready for that information frenzy—a disruptive force dominated by an evil entity. If that information had gotten out, especially at that period in time, the focus of society would have been on the dark world and the creatures of the night—the evil of the highest order. Extraterrestrial sounds terrible, and it was terrible what our government had to do in order to keep them a secret.

If JFK was set on releasing that information to the public, with no vow to every diplomatic means to stop it, our government had no choice left. The ramifications of going public with that information are what the devil wanted. There is nothing more disruptive at that time, except the second coming than an announcement by our government that an alien spacecraft had crashed on our shores. Every waking moment would have been spent on that. The world was never ready for that, and it never will be.

Fast-forward to a society in moral and social decline— a distracted world with an inclusive mindset for anything weird or perverted. They wouldn't just accept extraterrestrials; they would invite them home for dinner. Society and moral decline cannot stand for long. The moral fabric of society is fraying, and as it unravels, we are becoming more susceptible to the deceptions of the devil.

The distractions and desensitization have set the stage for the acceptance of these fallen beings. The church has failed to be the guiding light in this darkness. Instead of leading the charge against these deceptions, it has been complicit, either through silence or through misguided teachings. God's anger towards the church is justified.

The devil's plan has been cunning and methodical. By introducing advanced technology and then having it "discovered" through crashes, he has slowly acclimatized humanity to the idea of extraterrestrial life. Governments, driven by the desire to harness this technology, have kept secrets that have only served to deepen the deception.

As a society, we have embraced technology without questioning its origins. We have become so engrossed in our devices that we have lost sight of the spiritual battle being waged around us. The church needs to wake up and reclaim its role as the moral compass. It must remind the world that our struggle is not against flesh and blood but against the spiritual forces of evil.

There is still time to turn back to God to seek His guidance and protection. We must be vigilant, discerning the truth from the lies. We must not let ourselves be distracted by the shiny allure of technology or the false promises of these so-called extraterrestrials.

In the end, God's truth will prevail. The deceptions of the devil will be exposed, and his reign of terror will come to an end. Until that day, we must remain steadfast in our faith, unwavering in our commitment to God, and ever watchful of the schemes of the enemy.

Chapter 21

SOCIETY AT LARGE is breaking down. There is a falling away, and when our younger generations are not being taught, you can see it and feel it. We have lost several generations. I hope God will hold off His judgment for a time. Everybody, wake up. We, as a Christian nation, cannot stay on this terrible path. The societal norms that any decent society must have to survive—those lines are being crossed. An anesthetized and complacent society without moral absolutes is doomed to fail.

We, as humans, have no excuses. We have the light of God's grand and glorious creation. Put your devices down, go outside, get away from the city lights day or night, and just look around. Be honest with yourself. What you can see, hear, and smell is an undeniable and amazing creation that could only happen by a perfect and loving God. Most people who work outside and most of your rural people, like farmers and other trades that are out in the elements, know this. Those who hunt, fish, and camp more often—believers—can go into the woods, climb up in a deer stand, and look around as a testament to all who dare to believe.

The direction of our country and the world is on a very dangerous track. The reason why the word of God is a mystery and why things are written that way is simple: without the proper knowledge of the creation story, none of it would make any sense. Because now the seal has been broken, and the scroll is open. Put your devices down and look at what's going on around you. Heed the warning. It's going to be increasingly difficult to be a believer in the coming days because our younger generations are not being taught, and the breakdown of the family unit continues.

The church has let us down. If the church does not get back to the basics, the fundamentals of the faith, and stop all the manipulation and lies—no more showbiz Christianity—then we may get a respite. It has to come from God's people. God's hands are still raised high, and you better hope and pray they stay that way for a time. If the church does not get back to basics and do what it is supposed to do, then God will punish it severely. The erosion of the nuclear family and all the mixed messages coming from the church—it's no wonder attendance is at a record low. God is angry at the church.

If you pay attention to what is going on in the world, most of the ills are caused by the church. I hate to have to say that, but it's true. I've been saying to my family and friends for a long time that 98% of all preachers should be run off a cliff. I know that's a terrible thing to have to say. Listen, folks, we are running out of time. We cannot sugarcoat what is going on. You're seeing a rapid change in the world now, and it is not for the good.

If you and your family are believers, try and find a healthy, well-balanced church to attend. It won't be easy. A lot of those churches are manipulation zones, preying on vulnerable people's emotions. Many people are hurting and searching, and their emotions are toyed with for the gratification of the church. I've been in churches where the preacher tells the congregation not to be surprised if some people start speaking in tongues, setting the stage for manipulation and creating an environment of emotion.

We must seek out the truth and hold fast to it. The church must return to teaching the word of God in its purest form, without the added spectacle and manipulation. It is time to return to the basics, to the fundamental truths of our faith. We need to rebuild the family unit, strengthen our communities, and teach our children the ways of the Lord.

The church must humble itself before God and man, ask for forgiveness, change direction, and apologize to the world. Only then can we hope for a respite from God's judgment. We must humble ourselves and seek His guidance in all that we do. The moral and social decline of our society is a direct result of our straying from God's path.

It is up to us, the believers, to make a stand. We must be the light in this dark world. We must be the ones to teach the younger generations, to show them the truth of God's word, and to lead by example. We cannot rely on the church as it stands now; we must be the change we wish to see.

Let us pray for strength and guidance. Let us pray for our nation and our world. And let us pray for the church that it may return to its true calling and lead the way in these troubled times.

Chapter 22

SHORT-LIVED HIGH—YOU KEEP people vulnerable, preying on their emotions, manipulating them. You can make them do whatever you want. These are cults with a happy face. I've seen this garbage a thousand times, and I hate it. You toy with people's lives; this is serious business. This is life and death. You better be careful what you are doing to your flock. God isn't to be toyed with. There is still time to reverse course, but the people are waning. All the scandals you hear and read about—from pedophiles to miraculous claims like a woman's toes growing back—all these scandals are destroying the church. The church has become a mockery in the world.

The sentiment of our times should be a place of normalcy in a restless world, a sanctuary where believers and non-believers can congregate with their families and friends without their devices. A place where a family can all sit together, where we can look around and see other like-minded people who believe without all the nonsense. The church has got to get back to the basics. All the different programs and meetings and different services—Sunday night and Wednesday night services—can put too much stress on families. The family is the most important. The family is the bedrock of society, orchestrated by God. Your family comes first.

A healthy, well-balanced church is made up of like-minded families. Some churches put stress on families to be there every time the doors open. Don't fall for the manipulation. The Bible says, "Do not forsake the assembling of ourselves together" (Hebrews 10:25). It doesn't say to live there. Don't be manipulated otherwise. Make it a balance. Try to stay together as a family in the church. Don't separate yourselves. Sit together in church. If you miss a Sunday by sleeping in, that's OK. Wake up late, take your family out to breakfast or lunch. Don't feel guilty. You should enjoy going to church.

Believe me, we need the church. We need to see that we are not alone. When you and your family go to church, you set a tone and a message that you may not realize. There are friends and neighbors who see you and your family going to church; it's a wonderful testimony in and of itself. It is one of the things we do as believers that can have a profound effect on society for the good. Believe me, we need more of that. Please don't discount the value of the church. It is becoming more difficult to find a healthy, well-balanced church. A lot of churches are moving away from traditional services—that's a mistake.

If we, as believers, conduct ourselves in a righteous way—not a perfect way, but by our actions and the way we conduct ourselves in our daily lives—maybe just a smile and an encouraging word, we can change someone's life for the good. The church needs to get back to basics. I've stated it many times, and it is paramount. A lot of churches are getting away from the hymns, and I know why. You can slowly see what conformity does when you try to blend in with the world. The church must not conform to the world; it should be a sanctuary from the world.

The reason why churches are getting away from traditional hymns is because they make people uncomfortable. A lot of the traditional hymns are taken out of the Bible, and the word of God is powerful, and sometimes it pricks the heart. When you sit in church, and the word of God is opened up, if you are a non-believer and the hymns are sung and the word of God is preached, the burden that your heart and soul feel can be painful. The internal mechanisms given to us by God can be very uncomfortable. Some people like to call them the old hymns; just call them hymns. They should not be downplayed in any way.

A lot of churches are trying to force-feed modern music on us in our churches. I don't want to hear it in the church. I like a lot of different music on the radio—Christian, country, rock—but not in my church. Don't conform to the world. Be steadfast and basic. Stick with the fundamentals. The word of God is never changing; it is righteous and true. There's no reason why our music can't stay righteous and true. There's all kinds of crazy out there in the world; we don't need it in the church. People need a place to worship away from the whims of the world.

A lot of people thought that you need modern music to attract more youth—that is a misnomer, a failed experiment. Go back to basics. I've seen the experiment first-hand. I was looking for a window to jump out of. There are so many songs and hymns that never grow old. Don't conform to the world; let the world conform to you.

Chapter 23

REVERENT FEAR OF the Lord has subsided in our society—a very dangerous trend. Please put your devices down and look around. You need to focus on what is going on around you, your family, your schools, and your neighborhoods. Do you want your children or grandchildren to grow up in a godless society? If things don't change and we continue on this trajectory, and if the church doesn't step up to the plate and stop all the nonsense going on in the churches, we are seeing our world change right before our eyes. But there is hope. My mom quotes 2 Chronicles 7:14 all the time: "If my people, which are called by my name, shall humble themselves, and pray, and seek my face, and turn from their wicked ways; then I will hear from heaven, and will forgive their sin, and will heal their land."

We are at a crossroads as a nation. You can see it and feel it if you're paying attention. If you don't see what's going on, then you are distracted in a very dangerous scenario. You may think that I'm harping on the church. I am. There have been so many messages and so few ears. We have the roadmap—the Bible. All you have to do is read it. I never thought that I would be able to read it all. I've never read a complete book in my life, but when I started on this journey, I read the Bible—every word. It is the most amazing book ever written by far.

When I was pushed—well, when I had my feet kicked out from under me because I was too stupid to see the writing on the wall—I did not know at the time what I was supposed to do. When God wants you to do something, you will do it. I hope you understand that I'm not putting myself up on a pedestal. I should've been struck dead years ago by all the stupid things I did and said. We know that God uses some very strange folks sometimes.

One thing we can all agree on is that our world is changing, and not for the good. I believe we as a nation have a short window to reverse course—a respite for a time. I hate to be a spoiler, but if things don't change, we will be a part of the world to come, seeing the distracted society where everything goes. And you ain't seen nothing yet. You can watch what is on TV or the Internet, and all the cartoons that the kids and adults watch. Some of the weirdest things are cartoons, setting the stage and desensitizing the population to what is coming down the road—a weird and distorted view is what they want. They want everyone stuck on their devices, distracted from reality. They want everyone to stay inside their homes, away from the great outdoors, God's grand and glorious creation—a testament to God's handiwork.

For all the government has done, they have accomplished a monumental task of keeping the fallen angels—extraterrestrials—a secret. I do not know if, in the coming days, they will be revealed their true identity. Throughout history, most of the movies made about ET have been in an unfavorable light—from War of the Worlds to countless other movies portraying evil in the highest order. Their true colors will show. Everything they do is strategic because their time is short. The clock is ticking, and that's why things are ramping up.

The urgency of our situation cannot be overstated. Our society is moving away from God, and the church is failing to lead the way back to Him. The distractions of modern life, the over-reliance on technology, and the moral decline are all symptoms of a deeper spiritual malaise. We need to turn back to God, seek His face, and humble ourselves before Him. Only then can we hope to reverse the course we are on.

We must be vigilant in teaching our younger generations about the truths of the Bible. We must reinforce the importance of family, community, and faith. It is essential to break free from the grip of our devices and reconnect with the world around us. God's creation is a testament to His glory and a reminder of His presence in our lives.

The church must return to its roots, focusing on the fundamentals of the faith. It must be a place of refuge and strength, free from the distractions and manipulations that have plagued it. We need to reclaim our places of worship as sanctuaries from the world, where the word of God is preached, and the hymns of old are sung.

As individuals, we need to be the change we want to see. Our actions, our words, and our faith can have a profound impact on those around us. By living righteously and staying true to our beliefs, we can set an example that inspires others. The time is now to take a stand, to be vigilant, and to seek God's guidance in all that we do.

In the end, the truth will prevail. The deceptions of the devil will be exposed, and the glory of God will shine through. Let us pray for strength, wisdom, and discernment as we navigate these challenging times. Let us remain steadfast in our faith, ever watchful for the signs of the times, and always ready to do the work of the Lord.

Chapter 24

PLEASE DO NOT lose sight of what they are and where they came from. I wish I could tell you they are in our Earth-building wheelchairs for handicapped kids, but don't be naive. In the past, most portrayals—and rightly so—show them unfavorably. The tide is changing, casting them in a more favorable light just enough to pique your interest—a subtle manipulation by Hollywood for the realm of possibility. Oh, what a tangled web we weave. Between Hollywood and some in the church, there has never been a more destructive force on the planet.

You have to understand that the old devil is sneaky, and the stage is being set with all the movies that are out there, Congress having hearings on them, and the mainstream news talking about them. Even the military is releasing videos shot by pilots. To a desensitized population, it may not be a shocking revelation. Still, the mindset for most is that they would be from another planet and here to make trouble.

I'm going to give you another scenario: With the mindset that most beings are bad entities with a slight hint of some positive qualities for humanity, it wouldn't be too much of a push in any direction. No matter what direction the world takes or what you are told, they're fallen angels—the ones hurled to the Earth. Because they were once human and, after death, became angels, they now have the game figured out. They know how the game is played. There are many variables here, and the stage is already set for society to know about their existence. But will they be identified as the fallen ones, and would that cause chaos and disrupt society? It would probably cause excitement.

I may be a little "I told you so," but when the newness wears off, and the dust settles, people will want clarity. That's when it could become a sticky wicket. After the dust settles, there will have to be an explanation for all the true identities to come to light. With a distracted society, most people won't care either way. The ones who don't care will be giddy over it. Maybe just enough people will put it together when they slowly realize what is going on and the realization of what they are.

The unintended consequence is that enough people may start to speak out and ponder that there are things that go bump in the night. When their true identity is revealed—and that may take some time—the realization that they are evil will hit home. They are an evil entity living in our Earth. From the north, a measured and evil-minded approach has served them well for thousands of years. Satan knows his time is short. Their methodical degradation and degeneration of our society are apparent. The ball is rolling. Heed the warning. Stop and think about what is going on. Don't be stupid. You better cling to what is righteous and true—the word of God.

"To the inhabiters of the Earth and of the sea, for the devil is come down unto you, having great wrath, because he knoweth that he hath but a short time" (Revelation 12:12). The most shocking revelation will be that they have been here for thousands of years. In Job 1:6-7 (KJV), it says, "Now there was a day when the sons of God came to present themselves before the Lord, and Satan came also among them. And the Lord said unto Satan, Whence comest thou? Then Satan answered the Lord and said, From going to and fro in the earth, and from walking up and down in it."

The realization that these beings have been influencing humanity for millennia is both frightening and eye-opening. They have been here, manipulating and deceiving, walking among us. Their ultimate goal is to turn us away from God, to corrupt and destroy what is good and righteous.

As believers, we must remain vigilant and discerning. We must hold fast to the word of God, which is our ultimate guide and shield against these deceptions. The Bible is clear about the existence and influence of these fallen beings. It provides us with the knowledge and wisdom to navigate these perilous times.

We must also educate our children and future generations about these truths. It is crucial to pass down the knowledge of God's word and the reality of the spiritual battle we are in. We cannot allow them to be led astray by the false narratives and distractions of this world.

In the end, the truth will prevail. God's plan is unfolding, and no scheme of the devil can thwart it. The fallen angels will be exposed for what they truly are, and their reign of deception will come to an end. Until that day, we must remain steadfast in our faith, ever watchful, and always ready to stand against the forces of evil.

Chapter 25

IN THE KING James Version, it states, "The sons of God came to present themselves before the Lord." In the NIV, it states, "One day the angels came to present themselves before the Lord, and Satan also came with them." Remember, everything has to be looked at in proper context. If you're still in the mindset that the first created beings were with Adam and Eve going forward, then none of the scriptures will make sense to you, so you have to make jumps.

When they translated the King James Bible to the NIV, they did not understand in proper context who the sons of God were. Because we now know and understand who the sons of God are, that part of the mystery has been solved. Because the seal is broken and the scroll is open, the translators should not have changed the wording of the Bible in any way. What they did caused confusion. The word of

God is best left alone. In the King James Version, it states, "The sons of God came to present themselves before the Lord, and Satan also came among them."

At this time in history, the sons of God are the believers of the first created who have passed away and gone to heaven. Just because they're in heaven now does not mean they're angels. The way they conducted their lives first as humans on the earth may have something to do with whether they were chosen by God to be angels. There might be an angel boot camp. Before Satan was cast out of heaven, he spent a lot of his time sowing discord, accusing our brethren before God day and night. There is no love lost between God's angels and the devil and his angels; they are adversaries.

So, when Satan presented himself before the Lord, it was for manipulation purposes. He was probably hoping he could persuade a few more angels to come with him. Because the sons of God may not speak the language of angels, the sneaky devil would not be able to manipulate them. So, when the wording was changed in the NIV from "sons of God" to "angels," that should not have been done. God knew what He was doing when He wrote "the sons of God." The sons of God, in context, are not angels. In Hebrews 1:5, it says, "For to which of the angels did God ever say, 'You are my Son; today I have become your Father'? Or again, 'I will be his Father, and he will be my Son'?"

The devil and his angels have been slowly seeking recognition through many means. It has been playing out for many years in a methodical process that is picking up steam. Our government are trying to get ahead of the coming pressures from the dark side because our government, and possibly other governments, did not know that the crashes of spacecraft were a bold and strategic move by the devil. He wants recognition on his terms. All that technology will come with a price. The ball is slowly rolling into his court.

There will be a gradual overall acceptance of them or a grand gesture. If their overall view is moot, he can work with that. There could be another scenario to think about as a grand move. If the ETs are not pictured in a good light, at least they will be pictured with the press. The press is still press. You can see this taking all the oxygen out of the room. There will be a media frenzy like the world has never seen. The hearings and some in the media taking notice—the stage is being set. Our government, willing or unwilling, is playing ball. When you take a bite of the poisonous technology, sometimes just spitting it out won't do the trick.

The situation we find ourselves in is both complex and perilous. The devil's tactics are subtle and insidious, using the allure of advanced technology to entrap humanity. This technology reverse-engineered from the crashed spacecraft, is not just a marvel of engineering but a tool of deception. The devil's aim is to distract, to create dependency, and ultimately to control.

As believers, it is crucial to maintain a clear understanding of these times through the lens of Scripture. The word of God provides the context and the truth needed to navigate these deceptions. The confusion introduced by translating "sons of God" to "angels" in the NIV is a small but significant example of how misinterpretation can lead to misunderstanding.

We must remember that the fallen angels, the devil's agents, are not benevolent extraterrestrials here to guide or aid humanity. They are malevolent beings with a long history of rebellion against God. Their presence and influence in our world are part of a larger spiritual battle that has been ongoing since the beginning of time.

The modern portrayal of these beings in a more favorable light, whether through movies, media, or even some misguided teachings in the church, is part of the devil's strategy. By normalizing their presence and suggesting they may have positive qualities, the devil is preparing society for their eventual open acceptance.

However, we must remain vigilant. The true nature of these beings will eventually be revealed, and it will not be the benign, helpful entities that some portray. The realization that they are the fallen ones with a long history of malevolence will come as a shock to many. But by then, their influence may already be deeply embedded in society.

In this critical time, the role of the church is more important than ever. The church must return to the fundamentals of faith, grounding its teachings in the unaltered word of God. Believers must be equipped with the truth, able to discern the deceptions, and stand firm in their faith.

The societal acceptance of these beings, driven by a distracted and morally declining population, is a challenge we must face head-on. The church must speak out, educating its members about the true nature of the spiritual battle we are in. We must pray for wisdom, strength, and discernment as we navigate these times.

In conclusion, the world is at a pivotal point. The spiritual battle is intensifying, and the stakes are high. But we are not without hope. The word of God is our guide, and through it, we can find the truth and the strength to stand firm. Let us remain vigilant, ever-watchful, and committed to living out our faith in a world that desperately needs the light of Christ.

Chapter 26

*L*IKE I STATED before, when and if the dust set-tles, take notice and go towards the light. When you go towards the light, you will be given a little more light. You have to seek first the kingdom of God. The world would be very interested in who they are; the secret was so well kept for many years. Now is the time for the church, God's people, to step up to the plate. Stop all the nonsense and lies. Be straight with the world about what is going on. Do it with truth, by the word of God, and love.

The veil of secrecy is being lifted. The seal is broken, and the scroll is open. Now is not the time for confusion. Fill all the gaps with the word of God, or someone else will fill the gaps with lies. The old sneaky devil would have liked to see things play out on a more even keel for thousands and thousands of more years. When the Jewish people got their homeland back, which I mentioned before, it is no longer a small ball game.

They may say they're from another solar system. They may say they're here to help humanity. It's all lies. I hope that eventually, the reality of them being an evil entity, the fallen angels, will sink in. The only answer and the only truth is the written word. I hope people realize enough that all of this was foretold thousands of years ago in the word of God. The mystery is being revealed right before our eyes.

The warning for many people around the world will be a riveting time for a while. There will be nothing else talked about on the news and social media for a long time. That in and of itself is dangerous. Do not put blinders on. Look to your left and look to your right. Among all the confusion, stay calm. When all the confusion subsides— and it will take some time—the church has to finally step up to the plate. Don't let the world explain who they are. It should be handled with kid gloves, with truth and love.

You will now see why the word of God was written in very vague terms like "Giants." I've explained earlier in the book why things were worded that way because the Lord knew what would happen. You will see it play out right before your eyes. But now, the populations are largely desensitized. This is when all the confusion begins. The church has a short window to swoop in and answer all the questions with the word of God. Don't let the world put their spin on it. Among all the confusion is when we need more clarity.

Do not let a distorted and perverted view from some in the church say that they are the product of angels and humans who had sex. It's not possible and not true. They are among those of the first created—the sons of God in the beginning, possibly millions or billions of years before Adam. I've explained all this before, but this is a recap of the relevant time we are in. It is all starting to make sense now. The mystery is slowly being solved.

After their passing away, the believers received their celestial bodies. Immediately after death, because they were spirit-breathed—a spirit-body unity—they did not return to the ground as modern man does. They were caught up to the first heaven, where some become angels. Because Satan became dissatisfied and jealous, he began stirring up trouble in heaven. After war broke out, the devil and his followers lost their place in heaven, and they were cast down.

I've stated all this before, but you can now see what is going on in the world today, and the ETs being talked about openly. The stage is set for the revealing. You will hear all kinds of explanations about what they are and where they came from. Remember what they are: they are the fallen angels, evil of the highest order. There will be confusion and chaos, which the devil loves. Biblical clarity will be paramount.

Because of their portrayals in Hollywood and all the movies made about them in not the best light, people may be expecting the worst. Excitement will probably rule that day. It should be a time for retrospect. There may be storms on the horizon—mini storms indeed. Among all the chaos and excitement to come, don't be fooled because of the misdirection and complacency of the church. You are seeing the fruits of their labor.

God's people better start paying attention. Put your stupid cell phones down. Get your head out of the sand. Most countries around the globe do not worship the God of the Bible. The devil does not have to win them over. He doesn't care who you worship as long as you don't worship God. I've stated this before, and it's becoming more relevant now. The United States was founded on biblical Christian values—a beacon of light for the whole world to see. That has put a target on our back.

Among all the media frenzy to come, I hope the church, with moral clarity, will fill in all the gaps. We need to be prepared to step up and provide the truth. The church must rise to the occasion, rooted in the word of God, providing guidance and understanding. This is our moment to shine the light of God's truth into the darkness.

Let us be clear and steadfast in our message. The fallen angels are not benevolent beings. They are malevolent, deceptive, and dangerous. They have been orchestrating their plan for millennia, and now their time is running out. Their ultimate goal is to turn humanity away from God, to corrupt and destroy.

We must stand firm in our faith, armed with the word of God. We must teach our children and future generations the truths of the Bible. We must not let the world's narrative overshadow the truth. The church has a responsibility to lead, to provide clarity, and to uphold the truth.

In these times of great deception and confusion, let us hold fast to what is righteous and true. Let us remain vigilant, ever watchful, and ready to stand against the forces of evil. God is with us, and His truth will prevail.

Chapter 27

WITH THE MORAL decline of our nation and everyone stuck on their phones, Katie bar the door. They're looking for the next exciting thing. You have to remember one thing, and don't forget this: James 2:19 says, "Thou believest that there is one God; thou doest well: the devils also believe, and tremble." The devil and his angels will have their time in the limelight. Remember, one tree of sin only lasts a season.

I hope with the help of this little book, people will start to pay attention. Be very skeptical of what you are told by the media about who they are. The truth—that they are an evil entity that has been living in our earth for thousands of years—will not sit well. During a time of confusion and global unrest, many scenarios could play out. There will be enough confusion to go around to keep everyone guessing who they are. With chaotic scenes playing out globally, this is when the old sneaky devil may swoop in with all the answers.

I don't know about you, but I don't want to be hearing his rationale. If the church—that's a big if—uses this opportunity to evangelize, to explain to the people who they are and where they come from, I hope they don't sugarcoat the truth. If you look at what is going on in the world today, the way things are setting up, and you view everything with a biblical worldview, it is all making sense now.

Without acknowledgment of a pre-race of humans, none of it will make any sense to you. Because we know now that the pre-race is the sons of God and everything that entails, with that one part of the mystery solved, biblical clarity should rule the day. There will be millions of people who will be concerned and puzzled about who the ETs are. For those on the fence, not knowing or never thinking about a Higher Power before, this time could be very unnerving for them.

Just maybe they might put two and two together and seek the God of the Bible. The acknowledgment of an entity from our earth or from another planet, however, they spin it, might be a grand opportunity for evangelism. The truth will set you free, as they always say. Sometimes, the truth can be frightening. I'm not going to sugarcoat how horrifying they are.

Revelation 12:12 says, "Therefore rejoice, ye heavens, and ye that dwell in them. Woe to the inhabiters of the earth and of the sea! for the devil is come down unto you, having great wrath, because he knoweth that he hath but a short time." Those words should not be taken lightly. The Bible uses the word "woe" in this context, and it means grief. Their true colors may not shine through for a time. They should not be viewed with any light but only darkness—creatures of the night. There is nothing more terrifying and evil than the fallen ones.

Be very careful and suspect of what you see and hear about them in the coming days. They are doing things on our earth that are so horrifying that words cannot describe them. The chaos and confusion will muddy the waters. The word of God is the only clarity and truth you can depend on.

The church's opportunity for evangelism will be great. There will be many things among God's people that will be talked about in the coming days. Those who are still with me at this point in the book, what I have to talk about now is when many of you will part company with me.

We are entering a time when the truth will become more elusive and the lies more prevalent. The devil knows his time is short, and his deception is at an all-time high. As believers, we must stay rooted in the word of God and be prepared to stand firm in our faith.

The coming days will be a test of our resolve. There will be a push to accept these entities as benign or even beneficial to humanity. Do not be fooled. They are fallen angels, evil of the highest order, and their intentions are to lead humanity astray.

The confusion and chaos will be a breeding ground for deception. The devil will use every trick in his book to manipulate and control. But we have the word of God as our guide and our shield. We must use it to navigate these turbulent times.

This is not a time to be complacent. We must be vigilant, discerning, and unwavering in our faith. The world will be looking for answers, and we must be ready to provide them. We must speak the truth in love, but we must also be firm in our convictions.

We must also be prepared for the fact that many will reject the truth. They will be swayed by the lies and the allure of these beings. But we must continue to stand firm, knowing that we are fighting a spiritual battle that has eternal consequences.

In the end, the truth will prevail. God's plan will unfold, and the deception of the devil will be exposed. Until that day, we must remain steadfast, ever watchful, and committed to living out our faith in a world that desperately needs the light of Christ.

Chapter 28

IN THE COMING days, the narrative of the rapture of the church will be brought to the forefront. I believe that this narrative, taken for gospel and preached in most churches around the world, has had one of the most negative and devastating consequences for both the world and the church. In most churches, it is preached about in a pre-tribulation scenario, but most people don't realize it was never taught by the early churches. I believe some preachers had an epiphany in the 1800s and started this narrative. It has had some of the most devastating consequences on the church as a whole. When I hear it preached in churches today, it makes me sick. I don't like to be lied to.

There are quite a few passages that they jumble together to make their case. The most frequent ones they use are in 1 Thessalonians 4:13. In my NIV Bible, the heading for 1 Thessalonians 4:13 is "The Coming of the Lord." This NIV version was copyrighted in 1973, and it is the Zondervan Bible. In my Thompson Bible, the King James Version, first printed in 1908, states in the heading at the top of the page, "The Saints' Resurrection and Christ's Second Coming." The narrative of a pre-, mid-, or post-rapture of the church before the second coming of Christ is not true, and it doesn't even make sense.

A lot of people think it's not a big deal when the rapture is talked about. Well, when it is a lie and contrary to the word of God, it has caused a lot of problems with the church. The way it is talked about generally is that before things get bad—usually in a pre-trib scenario—believers will be taken away before the second coming of our Lord. Those who are hanging their hat on this narrative, thinking they're going to be taken away before things get really bad, are going to be very disappointed. We are headed in the wrong direction as a country, and it's going to get worse. We have a short window to reverse course and evangelize. Don't have the mindset that you're going to be raptured up before things get really bad—you're not.

If things don't change and we keep this trajectory, it's going to get so dark and ugly that you're not going to want to be a part of this world. Don't have the mindset that the coming is near, making God's people lazy and complacent. Only God Himself knows that day, not even the Son. When preachers talk about this, they think it is gospel. They tell their flock that before things get bad, things are going to get bad. If people don't get complacent and start evangelizing, they're sending the wrong message. The narrative of the rapture of the church has given God's people a false sense of security, and it is dangerous. It has given the mindset and false hope to millions of believers around the world.

When I realized that 1 Thessalonians 4:13 was about the second coming of the Lord, not some made-up rapture, it made a lot more sense. If that narrative of the pre-rapture of the church had not been taught by the mainstream church as a whole, the world could have been a different place. I've heard it explained six ways to Sunday, but the main theme is that God's people are going to be raptured up before things get bad. God is angry at His people. The church has let the world down with the mindset that we, as believers, are going to be taken away because we are not appointed to suffer wrath. It is giving a false sense of security, and it has made the church and God's people lazy.

It should be an ominous feeling in your gut that the church needs to get busy. We need God's people here on the earth right now to help in the coming days. God isn't done with the world yet. We have been telling people lies and giving them false hope, and that isn't the answer. The real answer lies in facing the truth and preparing ourselves for the trials that may come.

The early church never taught about a pre-tribulation rapture. Instead, they focused on enduring through tribulations and remaining faithful until the end. This message of perseverance and steadfast faith needs to be brought back to the forefront of our teachings. The idea that we will be whisked away before any trouble begins is not only misleading but also harmful. It has made many believers passive, expecting an escape instead of preparing for the possibility of enduring hardship.

Our world is changing rapidly, and not for the better. As believers, we have a responsibility to stand firm in our faith, to be the light in the darkness, and to spread the truth of God's word. This false narrative of a pre-tribulation rapture has lulled many into a false sense of security. It's time to wake up and realize that we may very well be called to endure through tough times.

We need to focus on strengthening our faith, building up our communities, and preparing our hearts and minds for whatever may come. This is not a message of despair but of hope and preparation. God's word equips us to face any challenge, but we must take it seriously and not be swayed by false teachings.

Let us return to the fundamentals of our faith, to the teachings of the early church, and to the truth of God's word. Let us be vigilant, watchful, and prepared. The trials and tribulations of this world are temporary, but our faith and the word of God are eternal. Let us hold fast to that truth and be ready to stand firm, no matter what comes our way.

Chapter 29

THERE SHOULD BE desperation among the church and God's people as a whole, not complacency. We have a short window to reverse course and apologize to the world for giving false hope. A lot of people will be angry with me for saying that and changing the narrative, but we don't have time to pussyfoot around. The lies have to stop. We, as Christians, are going to be planted here right along with everyone else.

You can sit on your hands and wait for some made-up rapture of the church, or you can set your sights on what is righteous and true—the second coming of the Lord. We, as God's people, are going to endure things on the earth right along with everyone else. It's going to get very uncomfortable to be a Christian in the coming days. You ain't seen nothing yet. I'm sorry that I have to tell you these things, but the world is rapidly changing, and not for the good.

The ETs have to ramp up their game; their time is short. I have stated this before if you have been around as long as they have, possibly millions of years, and you were seeing the end of the road, that's why things are moving along so quickly. If you block that garbage out of your mind about the rapture of the church, buddy, the world might look a little different. You might start to realize that time is of the essence.

The devastating effect that narrative has had on the church can't be measured. Everyone in my family believes in the rapture, even most of my friends. When you are told something from the pulpit, you want to believe it. Every word coming from man should be viewed with skepticism. The word of God is righteous and true. Test every word with that. You have to realize that most of the biblical world has been duped. I know this angers you and me—the first time I heard it, I was angry too.

You should have the mindset that there is no pre- or post-rapture of the church. It will serve you, your family, and the world as a whole in a much different light. It will give you a sense of urgency and a better perspective on how to deal with the world. When we are in it for the long haul, if things stay at this clip and God's people don't evangelize with a sense of urgency, the world will become like it was in the days of Noah.

The rapture of the church is a misnomer. Completely blot it out of your mind. It will force you and your family to look at things differently—the way God intended. With that gone out of your mind now, I hope it will take some distant memory and clear with the realization that things are headed in the wrong direction rapidly. Don't take what you see and hear lightly anymore. Pay attention because we have lost such valuable time thinking we were going to be raptured up before things go haywire.

It is time to be bold now. With the stage set, everyone stuck on their devices, and the media storm with the announcement of the ETs, this is when the erosion of civil liberties can happen right under our noses. Buyer beware. Change your mindset that Christ is not coming back for hundreds of years. We're going to be a part of this world whether we like it or not. Because the church has been complacent, we have a lot of ground to make up for. It has to come from God's people, and it has to start now. The road is narrowing.

We need to take action immediately. God's people must rise to the occasion and start evangelizing with fervor. This is not a time for sitting back and waiting for an escape. This is a time for engagement, for spreading the truth of God's word, and for preparing ourselves and others for the trials ahead.

The church has a critical role to play in these times. It must become a beacon of truth and hope, standing firm on the word of God and rejecting false narratives. It must support its members in understanding the true nature of the times we are living in, providing guidance and encouragement for the journey ahead.

We must also look at our own lives and ask ourselves if we are living in a way that honors God and prepares us for what is to come. Are we focused on the temporary comforts of this world, or are we storing up treasures in heaven? Are we complacent in our faith, or are we actively seeking to grow closer to God and spread His love to those around us?

It is not enough to simply wait for the end. We must be active participants in God's plan, working to bring as many people as possible into His kingdom. This is our calling and our mission. We must be vigilant, discerning, and unwavering in our faith.

The time for complacency is over. We must recognize the urgency of the times we are living in and respond accordingly. Let us be bold in our faith, steadfast in our convictions, and committed to living out the truth of God's word in every aspect of our lives.

Chapter 30

KNOW THAT MY telling all of you about the fake narrative of the rapture of the church will not sit well. We have to get busy. God's people have to spread the gospel with a new perspective on life here on earth. A bold direction for a drastic change in our mindset. We have a desire as believers to go home, to be caught up to meet the Lord in the air at the second coming. That's instilled in all who believe. But we are here and now. We have a job to do. The road is narrow, and we have a short window. It is up to us as believers to shepherd the lost. If we don't seize this opportunity in a time of need and want, then someone else will fill in the gap.

There are going to be a lot of questions put forth in the coming days. If you look at things now, realizing that Christ's return is in the distant future and that we are headed down a long and narrow road right along with everyone else—that's the way we should've been looking all along. The false narrative of a rapture has caused a lot of damage, and we have a lot of ground to make up. The answers coming from the world will not serve us. With all the distractions out there, it's not going to be easy. The old sneaky devil and his angels are going to relish all the attention. We cannot let them narrate who they are. We must be prepared for every scenario.

The devil and his angels have had a long time to prepare for this moment. There will be all kinds of sneaky and manipulative reasons given for their existence. They might even play the victim card, trying to tug at everyone's heartstrings with the poor pitiful me scenario. They will take time and all the oxygen out of the room. From one end of the spectrum to the other, everything has to be vetted with the word of God. The church has to seize this opportunity. It has to be straight with the world and tell everyone what they are—fallen angels. These are beings that God, the Creator of the universe, cast out thousands of years ago.

I hope people start to realize that with the knowledge of an evil entity, there is a higher power—a grand Creator who created everything for good for His divine purpose. The grand and glorious plan laid out in the word of God for the whole world to see is happening right before our eyes. The seal is broken, and the scroll is open. With all the mysterious things to see in the coming days, there has to be a stark realization of good and evil. The good radiates from the Most High and from the one true God, the beginning and the end, the first and the last, our Heavenly Father. Or you can choose the one out of the bowels of hell—from the north, a dark and hidden world, gloomy and unknown, a covering over to hoard a reserve for evil, a place to look, a secret place in our earth.

The gift of free will is that everyone has to make a choice. With the rapid pace our world is changing, you better pick a side. I hope we get a time of reprieve in our country, a respite, and an awakening. The excitement of their existence for many in the coming days will slowly subside. The explanation of who and what they are and where they came from will take less convincing for the world than it will for the church. When the church realizes that they are wrong about the beginning, the pre-Adamic race, they will have to bow their necks.

The truth is a powerful thing. Once it is known, it cannot be unknown. The realization that the narrative of the rapture has been a distraction will hit hard. But it is necessary for us to move forward. We have to embrace the truth and let it guide us in these tumultuous times. The church must acknowledge its mistakes, seek forgiveness, and correct its course. Only then can we hope to be the beacon of light that the world so desperately needs.

We have a lot of work to do. The time is now. We must spread the gospel with urgency and clarity. We must be prepared to answer the difficult questions and provide the truth that the world is seeking. The devil's lies have been pervasive, but God's truth is enduring. We must stand firm in our faith, unwavering in our mission, and resolute in our commitment to God's word.

Let us not be complacent. Let us rise to the occasion, knowing that we are equipped with the truth of God's word. The world is watching, and it is up to us to provide the answers. The road ahead is challenging, but with God's guidance and our unwavering faith, we can navigate it together.

In conclusion, we must reject the false narrative of the rapture and embrace the truth of God's word. We must evangelize with urgency, knowing that time is of the essence. We must prepare ourselves and others for the trials ahead, standing firm in our faith and spreading the gospel. The world is in need of the truth, and it is up to us to provide it.

Chapter 31

A DEEP AND PROFOUND review of the creation of our universe from a purely biblical perspective will be in order. I know this will be hard to swallow for many, especially in the church. The world will be open to any explanation, and that is dangerous. We cannot allow this to become misconstrued. The world will try to make this very perplexing, but it is not. A confusing scenario will serve the ETs much better than the truth. If they can keep the population at large, guessing who and what they are, their work will be much easier. Sunlight is a good disinfectant. We have to seize the opportunity with salt and light. God is not the author of confusion—the devil and his angels are.

The cat is out of the bag, and the veil of secrecy is lifted. The church has to pounce immediately. It cannot let confusion rule the day. There's too much at stake.

If things are handled properly with the broad swath of the electorate, just maybe a grand awakening can happen with biblical truths. Because when all this starts to shake out with the reality of an evil entity, there has to be a reality of a good entity. I hope people, God's people, and the church will do some soul-searching. We have a short window as God's people to get our house in order before the coming chaos. A distracted and confused house cannot stand. A truthful and calming voice from God's people can tame the raging seas.

The world is watching this play out in the media now, with hearings taking place on Capitol Hill. You can tell there's a lot of interest in the news. There's still a lot of skepticism, with most people around the world wondering what they may be. The Band-Aid is slowly being removed. Dumping a pile of crap doesn't help; it just spreads the smell around. When the ETs are finally made known, there will be a media frenzy around the world, and there will be nothing else talked about in the news for a long time. Be very careful of what you see and hear. There will be a lot of different reactions to what is taking place. Among some of the chaos is when you really have to be on guard.

Eventually, in the coming days, there will be a day of reckoning, and an explanation from some Washington bureaucrat will not be sufficient. The truth of what they are will be shocking. It will be hard to swallow among those in the church. Reality will eventually sink in. The truth will be an uphill climb with most of the world. After this starts shaking out, there will be a lot of people who will not like the biblical view of what they are and where they came from because of their origin and their true nature. The only rational truth will come from the word of God.

Eventually, they will have to admit and realize that there is a divine Creator, the true God. This could change the narrative with many people around the world, and they just might give God a second look. Like in a time of need or crisis, as the old saying goes, there are no atheists in the trenches. When your back is against the wall, and things start shaking out, and you're praying to your Mother Nature, false god, with no effect—today, when it comes down to the nut-cutting, most people cry out, "Lord, Lord, the God of Abraham, Isaac, and Jacob."

I know that this is a lot to swallow and completely different than what you've been taught. But now is the time for clarity and truth. We must rely on the word of God as our guiding light. The narrative the world will spin will be confusing and misleading, but we have the ultimate truth in the Bible. We must prepare ourselves to answer the tough questions, to provide clarity in the midst of chaos, and to be the voice of reason and truth.

The church has an unprecedented opportunity to lead, to be the light in a dark world, and to bring people to the knowledge of the true God. This is a pivotal moment in history, and we must not squander it. We must stand firm in our faith, unwavering in our commitment to the truth, and bold in our proclamation of the gospel.

The days ahead will be challenging, but we are equipped with the word of God. Let us move forward with confidence, knowing that we are on the side of truth and righteousness. Let us be the salt and light in the world, guiding others to the truth and showing them the way to the true God.

In conclusion, we must reject the lies and confusion of the world and embrace the truth of God's word. We must evangelize with urgency, knowing that time is of the essence. We must prepare ourselves and others for the trials ahead, standing firm in our faith and spreading the gospel. The world is in need of the truth, and it is up to us to provide it.

Chapter 32

WE HAVE TO live our lives day-to-day. We are in the here and now. Every made-up whim of doctrine will come and go, but if you do not see the writing on the wall and the stage is being set, then you and your family and friends need to stop, put your devices down, take a pause, and really look at what's going on in our country. If you deny or make excuses for what you are hearing and seeing, it will be at your own peril.

If you're being honest with yourself, did you ever think you would see the day when men would be competing in women's sports, blurring the lines between male and female? This is just the beginning. If you do not have moral absolutes in a society, it is doomed for failure. When you can blur the lines and make everything fuzzy in our society—no right or wrong, up means down, right means left—you have set the stage for any scenario they want.

You can no longer sit on your hands and wait for the rapture. If you care about your children and your grandchildren, and so on and so forth, we can take this opportunity to evangelize.

With all the distractions out there in our world today, and you throw the ETs in the mix and all the mixed messages coming from the church, it is no wonder that there's so much confusion in the world today. The church has to go back to the basics. It has to be a place of reverence and normalcy, a sanctuary. Every believer needs a place to go without all the distractions in their day-to-day lives. I've talked about some of the nuttiness that has gone on in the churches in this book already. With the way things are playing out in society, the church has to trust and obey.

If you do not believe in the power of our Lord Jesus Christ and the Holy Bible, God's written word, then you need to find something else to do. People, you have to understand we are headed down a narrow road. There is still time, but only a short time. I've stated this before, but I'm gonna say it again. The world and society at large are in the shape they're in because of the failure of the church. Go back to the basics. You have to believe in your heart. When the word of God is preached by a man who believes every word, there is nothing more powerful than that.

I know I've gone back to the insufficiency of the church. Back in the time of Christ, the church was only worried about the church, not the lost. They were called identity thieves, and their leaderships were scorned. They were full of dead men's bones, and their self-righteous works were as filthy rags. The strongest emotive words used to describe the church and the leadership of the day without cursing. Because we have the blueprint from the beginning all the way to the end and everything in between, eventually, things start to move and move quickly.

The mystery of it all is being revealed right before our eyes. You can go through life believing in God or not believing; it is your choice. Just look at it in a sense—why take the chance? If you believe that God sent His son Jesus Christ, and you ask Him to come and live in your heart, and you are baptized for remission, then one day you will have eternal life. If you are someone who is on the fence, not really knowing or believing there is a God, and you or your family haven't been raised in a healthy, well-balanced church, but you see things out in society that you don't understand and like, if you rationally and calmly think to yourself, what would be the harm in becoming a believer?

Just think about it in a practical sense—why take the chance? If you are a free-thinking person and you never really thought about life and death, but you and your family are seeing things playing out in society that are giving you pause, the moral decline is apparent. Especially if you have children and grandchildren, things are rapidly changing, and not for the good.

Let's just say you go all the way—accept, believe, repent, and be baptized for remission. You and your family live your lives in a way that is pleasing to God. But when that day comes, and you pass away, and there is no heaven, and there is no hell, and everything you've been taught and believed doesn't come true, and life just stops. Maybe in hindsight, we can say living as a believer had some challenges and struggles, but all in all, there was really no harm in that.

What about the people who roll the dice, those who take the chance and live without faith? They live as if there is no higher power, no divine Creator, no moral absolutes. When their time comes, if they are wrong, the consequences are eternal. The stakes are too high to gamble with your soul. The truth of God's word offers a clear path, a foundation for life that provides hope and purpose.

Now is the time for a decision. We must choose whom we will serve. As for me and my house, we will serve the Lord. The urgency of the moment cannot be overstated.

We must evangelize, teach, and live out our faith boldly. The world is watching, and they need the truth more than ever. The lines are being drawn, and we must stand firm on the side of righteousness.

The road is narrowing, and the time is short. Let us rise to the challenge, be the light in the darkness, and guide as many as we can to the truth of God's word. Our lives, our actions, and our faith must reflect the love and truth of Jesus Christ. Let us not be found wanting when the final tally is made. Stand firm, be courageous, and trust in the Lord with all your heart.

Chapter 33

*I*F YOU DECIDE to go the way of the world, to do it your own way, and take the chance, I want you to think about the ramifications of that. What if it is all true? Every word of the Bible is true, and you and your family live your lives in a secular way. There is a 100% chance that you're going to pass away sometime in your life. You roll the dice and do it your way, but in the end—and the end will come—that chance granted to you and everyone else on the planet by free will, your choice, your decision.

Because you went the way of the world, you lived your life the way you wanted. You might have been a good person and upstanding in your community. You put your trust in humanity and the environment and worried about what men might think of you and your family. You only feared what man can do or say or what society at large thinks. You've taken the chance. You've rolled the dice. You've done everything the world expected of you. "I did it my way."

But you should not be afraid of those who can kill the body and after that have no more that they can do. But I will warn you whom you shall fear: fear Him who, after He has killed, has the power to cast into hell. Yes, I tell you, fear Him. Through the power of God, Luke 12:4-5 says: "Man can only do so much. It all plays out in the end, and none of it turns out to be true, but we lived our lives a good way to help all humanity." That is a good thing. I beg you, don't take that chance. The evidence of a divine Creator is overwhelming. It is your choice.

The ultimate love granted to us by God is free will. We know all the challenges that come with that gift. Do you want someone to love you because they are programmed to love you, or do you want them to love you by their own free will? God will look upon us with great love and great joy. We came to Him without seeing Him, by faith. Because of free will, we chose that narrow path through our Lord and Savior, Jesus Christ. God will stand and overlook His glorious kingdom, and He will say, "I am well pleased."

When many of you go back and read Genesis again, you may say to yourselves, "How did I miss that?" Remember, it was always there, but it was not in God's perfect timing until now. There are many who have taken a bite of the poisonous fruit; you better spit it out and take from the tree of life. There is still time.

They are rejected silver because the Lord has rejected them. The seal is broken and the scroll is open, and now is the time for clarity and action. God's word has always been clear, and the path to salvation has always been through faith in Jesus Christ. There are no shortcuts, no alternative routes. The broad road leads to destruction, but the narrow path, though difficult, leads to eternal life.

We live in a world where every whim and doctrine can sway us. The confusion of our times is a testament to the necessity of firm, unchanging truth. The Bible provides that truth. It stands as a beacon of light in a dark world, guiding us, teaching us, and calling us back to the basics of faith.

This moment in history is critical. We have a short window to make a difference, to correct our course, and to lead others to the truth. The church must rise to the occasion. We must be vigilant, discerning, and unwavering in our faith. We must reject the lies of the world and embrace the eternal truths of God's word.

If you are on the fence, now is the time to decide. If you have been swayed by the world, now is the time to return to the truth. If you have taken the path of least resistance, now is the time to stand firm and choose the narrow road. The consequences of your choice are eternal. Choose wisely.

In conclusion, I urge you to take a deep, introspective look at your life. Evaluate your beliefs, your actions, and your path. Turn to the Bible, seek God's guidance, and commit to living a life that honors Him. There is no greater calling, no greater purpose, and no greater reward.

To follow Rick:
ricknehrt.com.